Exemplar Hiberniae

100 Years of Local Government in County Wexford

Compiled by

William P Creedon

EXEMPLAR HIBERNIAE

100 Years of Local Government in County Wexford

Compiled by

William P Creedon

First published 1999 by Institute of Public Administration
for
Wexford County Council

57-61 Lansdowne Road
Dublin 4

© Wexford County Council and
William P Creedon 1999

All rights reserved. No part of this publication may be reproduced or transmitted in any form or by any means, electronic or mechanical, including photocopy, recording or any information storage and retrieval system, without permission in writing from the publisher.

ISBN 1 902448 13 8

British Library Cataloguing in Publication Data
A catalogue record of this book is available from the British Library

Design by David Cooke
Origination by Wendy A Commins, The Curragh
Printed by Criterion Press Limited

CONTENTS

	Foreword	viii
	Chairmen and vice-chairmen 1899-1999	1
Chapter 1	Local government in the nineteenth century	7
Chapter 2	The Local Government Act of 1898	15
	The last grand jury for fiscal purposes	18
Chapter 3	The elections of 1899	19
Chapter 4	The first meeting of the council	25
Chapter 5	One hundred years of local government – a manager's perspective	31
Chapter 6	Views from the council chamber	51
	County council members: photographs	53
Chapter 7	County managers	61
	List of county managers and other officers	73
Chapter 8	Working for the council	75
	County council staff at present: photographs	83
	County council staff at 31 December 1998	95
	Former employees	100
Appendix I	Council elections and schedules of members	103
	Proportional representation	108
	County Hall, Wexford	121
Appendix II	Rural district councils 1899	123
Appendix III	Chronology	127
	Vehicle registration in County Wexford	133
Appendix IV	Wexford County Council archives	169
Appendix V	Wexford County Council publications – a select bibliography	171

Acknowledgements and photo credits

Wexford County Council acknowledges with thanks the many individuals and organisations that supported this work, in particular Carmel O'Shea and Mary Olive Harpur who indexed the council minute books, Jarlath Glynn, Billy Ringwood, Kathleen Lucking, Kevin Hurley, Gerry Forde Snr, Bernard Browne, Róisín Leahy, Evelyn Nolan, Brendan Underwood, Dr Austin O'Sullivan, Anne Ahearn, Anna Kinsella, Tom Williams, Liam Morris, and the staffs of the National Archives of Ireland, Wexford County Council and Wexford Public Libraries.

The publishers wish to thank the following for their kind permission to reproduce illustrative material in this book: Edward Carroll, Peggy and Tony Cronin, Sheila Crosbie, Virginia Crossman, Bridie Doyle, B T G Esmonde, Sean and Anne Foley, Joe Funge, Nicholas Furlong, Frank Murphy, Hilary Murphy, Michael Nolan, Dr Austin O'Sullivan, Padge Reck, Josephine Sullivan, Wexford County Council Archives, and Wexford County Library Archives. All possible care has been taken to trace copyright holders. If any errors or omissions have been made, please notify the publishers so that corrections can be made in subsequent editions.

The County Hall

FOREWORD

WEXFORD PEOPLE have a long tradition of pride in their locality, its traditions, history and cultural values. Every year an extensive range of publication – histories, yearbooks, journals, diaries – add to our understanding of the development of our county.

A progressive force within that development over the past one hundred years has been Wexford County Council. Its services have benefited every man, woman and child in the county over generations. Today, Wexford County Council is a sophisticated organisation with an extensive range of responsibilities, but many will remember when surfaced roads, piped water and sewerage schemes for villages and rural parishes were ambitious goals. We have come a long way.

We have come a long way thanks to the dedication and enthusiasm of generations of elected members and officials working closely with local communities to make our model county a special place in which to live. Operating under the aegis of the Department of the Environment and Local Government, whose support we gratefully acknowledge, the contribution of the council in the delivery of essential infrastructure, and in the provision of leadership to initiate and drive innovative projects, should not be underestimated. The dynamic relationships that exist between councillors representing local communities and officials offering expertise and service management has been central to the economic and cultural progress we have achieved in County Wexford. Success has been built on the strong partnerships that the council has developed with the local communities. These partnerships, and the strategic alliances that have also been fostered with state agencies and other organisations, will continue to underpin the development of County Wexford as we face the challenges of the future.

In this year when we celebrate one hundred years of local government in Ireland, it is appropriate that we acknowledge the achievements of Wexford County Council to date. We are delighted that Wexford County Council has prepared this book. Researcher, author and compiler, William P Creedon, has brought to its production the care and attention that he brought to his duties as county secretary from 1970 to 1995. In compilation he was assisted ably by Celestine Rafferty from the council's public library service, whose commitment to the project has been impressive. Thanks are due also to council staff members, Fionnuala Hanrahan, Tony Larkin and Cathy Kirby. Wexford County Council also acknowledges with thanks the many individuals and organisations that supported this work.

Undoubtedly, *Exemplar Hiberniae: 100 Years of Local Government in County Wexford* will be an important addition to the record of County Wexford as well as to the literature of public service in Ireland.

Leo Carthy, Chairman

Leo Carthy
Chairman
Wexford County Council
May 1999

Seamus Dooley
County Manager

RÉAMHRÁ

Tá traidisiún fada mórtais ag muintir Loch Garman, ina gceantar féin agus i stair, traidisiúin agus luachanna cultúrtha an cheantair sin. Gach uile bhliain, cuirtear lenár dtuiscint ar fhás agus ar fhorbairt ár gcontae, trí réimse leathan foilseachán – stair áitiúil, irisí, bliainirisí agus dialanna.

D'fheidhmigh Comhairle Chontae Loch Garman mar fhórsa forásach sa bhforbairt sin, le céad bliain anuas. Thar na glúine ó shin, bhain fir, mná is páistí tairbhe as seirbhísí na comhairle. Sa lá atá inniu ann, is foras sofaisticiúil é Comhairle Chontae Loch Garman le réimse leathan freagrachtaí. Ach beidh cuimhne ag go leor daoine ar an tráth nach raibh i mbóithre le dromchla ceart, uisce curtha trí phíopaí, agus scéimeanna séarachais do shráidbhailte agus do pharóistí tuaithe, ach sprioc uaillmhianach. Tá turas fada déanta ó shin againn.

Tá aistear fada déanta againn, a bhuí le dúthracht agus le díograis na nglún de bhaill tofa agus d'oifigigh, a d'oibrigh go dlúth le pobail áitiúla, ar mhaithe le hionad maireachtála speisialta a chruthú ins an gcontae eiseamlárach seo againn féin. Ní cóir rannpháirtíocht na comhairle i soláthar bonneagair riachtanaigh, agus an chinnireacht a thug sí i dtionscnaimh agus i dtiomáint tionscadal nuálach, a mheas faoina luach. Tá an chomhairle ag feidhmiú faoi scáth na Roinne Comhshaoil agus Rialtais Áitiúil, agus is mór againn a tacaíocht. Tá gaol dinimiciúil idir na comhairleoirí a dhéanann ionadaíocht ar son na bpobal áitiúil agus na hoifigigh a thairgíonn saineolas agus bainistíocht seirbhíse, agus tá an gaol seo lárnach don bhforbairt eacnamúil agus chultúrtha atá bainte amach againn i gContae Loch Garman. Tá an dea-thoradh atá bainte amach tógtha ar na comhpháirtnéireachtaí láidre atá forbartha ag an gcomhairle leis na pobail áitiúla. Beidh na comhpháirtnéireachtaí seo agus na comhaontais straitéiseacha a forbraíodh le forais stáit agus le háisíneachtaí eile, ag cur taca faoi fhorbairt Chomhairle Chontae Loch Garman agus sinn ag tabhairt aghaidhe ar an dúshlán na todhchaí.

Seamus Dooley, Co. Manager

Táimid ag ceiliúradh céad bliain den rialtas áitiúil in Éirinn, agus tá sé tráthúil go dtabharfaimís aitheantas don saothar iontach atá déanta ag Comhairle Chontae Loch Garman go dtí seo. Is é Liam Ó Críodáin an taighdeoir, an t-údar agus an tiomsaitheoir, agus rinne sé an saothar seo leis an gcúram céanna agus leis an aire chéanna lenar chomhlíon sé a dhualgais mar rúnaí contae ó 1970 go dtí 1995. Chabhraigh Celestine Rafferty ó sheirbhís leabharlainne poiblí na comhairle leis ins an tiomsú agus thug sí faoin tionscnamh le díograis a bhí suntasach. Tá buíochas ag dul do bhaill eile d'fhoireann na comhairle freisin, Fionnuala Hanrahan, Tony Larkin agus Cathy Kirby. Gabhann Comhairle Chontae Loch Garman buíochas le mórán daoine agus eagraíochtaí a thug a dtacaíocht don obair seo.

Cuirfidh *Exemplar Hiberniae: 100 Years of Local Government in County Wexford* go mór, gan amhras ar bith, leis an gcuntas ar Chontae Loch Garman agus leis an litríocht ar an tseirbhís phoiblí in Éirinn.

Leo Carthy	Seamus Dooley
Cathaoirleach	Bainisteoir Contae
Comhairle Chontae Loch Garman	
Bealtaine 1999	

Wexford County Council coat of arms – granted by the Chief Herald of Ireland, July 1988. The shield of arms has been devised to reflect the topography, history and people of County Wexford. The basic colours, purple and gold, are the sporting colours of the county. The wavy band represents the River Slaney which flows through the county from north to south and has its estuary in Wexford Harbour. The spearheads call to mind the Laigin or Leinster people, so called because of the laighne or spears with which they were armed when they first landed in what is now County Wexford in the third century BC.

The main motif of the shield represents the lighthouse at Hook Head and the upstanding lion armed with a pike symbolises Wexford's part in the 1798 Rebellion.

The motto, Exemplar Hiberniae, translates as 'a model for Ireland', the description by which Wexford is well known throughout Ireland – the Model County.

CHAIRMEN AND VICE-CHAIRMEN 1899-1999

	Chairman	Vice-chairman		Chairman	Vice-chairman
1899	Sir Thomas H G Esmonde, Bart	Edmond Hore	1923	Edward P Foley	John Cummins
1900	Sir Thomas H G Esmonde, Bart	Edmond Hore	1924	Edward P Foley	John Cummins
1901	Sir Thomas H G Esmonde, Bart	Edmond Hore	1925	Thomas McCarthy	Col. C M Gibbon
1902	Sir Thomas H G Esmonde, Bart	Edmond Hore	1926	Thomas McCarthy	Col. C M Gibbon
1903	Sir Thomas H G Esmonde, Bart	Edmond Hore	1927	Thomas McCarthy	Col. C M Gibbon
1904	Sir Thomas H G Esmonde, Bart	Edmond Hore	1928	Michael Doyle	James Shannon
1905	Sir Thomas H G Esmonde, Bart	M A Ennis	1929	Michael Doyle	Col. C M Gibbon
1906	Sir Thomas H G Esmonde, Bart	M A Ennis	1930	Michael Doyle	Col. C M Gibbon
1907	Sir Thomas H G Esmonde, Bart	M A Ennis	1931	Michael Doyle	James E Walsh
1908	Sir Thomas H G Esmonde, Bart	M A Ennis	1932	Michael Doyle	James E Walsh
1909	Edmond Hore	Charles H Peacocke	1933	Michael Doyle	James E Walsh
1910	Edmond Hore	Charles H Peacocke	1934	Denis Allen	Richard Corish
1911	John Bolger	Charles H Peacocke	1935	Denis Allen	Richard Corish
1912	John Bolger	Charles H Peacocke	1936	Denis Allen	Richard Corish
1913	John Bolger	Charles H Peacocke	1937	Denis Allen	Richard Corish
1914	John Bolger	Charles H Peacocke	1938	Denis Allen	Richard Corish
1915	John Bolger	Charles H Peacocke	1939	Denis Allen	Richard Corish
1916	John Bolger	Charles H Peacocke	1940	Denis Allen	Richard Corish
1917	John Bolger	Michael Doyle	1941	Denis Allen	Richard Corish
1918	John Bolger	Michael Doyle	1942	Denis Allen, July to Sept. '42	Richard Corish
1919	John Bolger	Michael Doyle	1942	Richard Corish, from 2 Sept. '42	Thomas McCarthy
1920	John R Etchingham	Dr James Ryan	1943	Denis Allen	Thomas McCarthy
1921	John J O'Byrne	Edward P Foley	1944	Denis Allen	Thomas McCarthy
1922	John R Etchingham	Edward P Foley	1945	Denis Allen	Thomas McCarthy

**Sir Thomas H Grattan Esmonde, Bart,
Chairman 1899-1909**

Edmond Hore J P, Chairman 1909-1911

John Bolger, Chairman 1911-1920

	Chairman	Vice-chairman		Chairman	Vice-chairman
1946	Denis Allen	Thomas McCarthy	1973	Michael Hart	Pat McDonald
1947	Denis Allen	Thomas McCarthy	1974	Andrew Doyle	James J Bowe
1948	Denis Allen	Seán O'Byrne	1975	Seán Browne TD	James J Bowe
1949	Denis Allen	Seán O'Byrne	1976	James J Bowe	Pat McDonald
1950	James Sinnott	James J Bowe	1977	Leo Carthy	James J Bowe
1951	James J Bowe	James Sinnott	1978	Thomas Howlin	Leo Carthy
1952	John O'Leary TD	James J Bowe	1979	Thomas Howlin	Leo Carthy
1953	James J Bowe	John O'Leary TD	1980	John Roche	James Curtis
1954	Peter Dempsey	James J Bowe	1981	John Roche	James Curtis
1955	James J Bowe	John O'Leary TD	1982	Michael D'Arcy	Leo Carthy
1956	James J Kennedy	Seán Browne	1983	James Curtis	Patrick Codd
1957	James J Kennedy	Timothy F D'Arcy	1984	Pat Codd	Michael Sinnott
1958	James J Bowe	John O'Leary TD	1985	Thomas Howlin	James Curtis
1959	James J Kennedy	James Galvin	1986	James Curtis	Michael Sinnott
1960	James J Bowe	Leo Carthy	1987	Michael Sinnott	Lorcan Allen
1961	James J Kennedy	Leo Carthy	1988	Lorcan Allen	Rory Murphy
1962	Thomas F Byrne	Leo Carthy	1989	Rory Murphy	Hugh Byrne
1963	James J Bowe	Leo Carthy	1990	Hugh Byrne	Gus Byrne
1964	Thaddeus J O'Loughlin	Leo Carthy	1991	Gus Byrne	Michael D'Arcy
1965	James J Kennedy	Leo Carthy	1992	Jim Walsh	James Curtis
1966	Thomas F Byrne	Leo Carthy	1993	Michael D'Arcy	Michael Sinnott
1967	James J Bowe	Leo Carthy	1994	James Curtis	Michael Sinnott
1968	Thomas F Byrne	Thaddeus J O'Loughlin	1995	Rory Murphy	Lorcan Allen
1969	James J Bowe	Martin Dunbar	1996	Lorcan Allen	Hugh Byrne
1970	Thomas F Byrne	Michael D'Arcy	1997	John A Browne TD	Gus Byrne
1971	Michael D'Arcy	Martin Dunbar	1998	Leo Carthy	Seán Doyle
1972	Thomas F Byrne	Michael Hart			

John R Etchingham, Chairman
1920-1921; 1922-1923, died 23 April 1923

John J O'Byrne, Chairman 1921

Edward P Foley, Chairman 1923-1925

CHAIRMEN AND VICE-CHAIRMEN 1899-1999

Thomas McCarthy, Chairman 1925-1928

Michael Doyle, Chairman 1928-1934

Denis Allen, Chairman 1934–September 1942; 1943-1950

Richard Corish, Chairman September 1942-1943

James Sinnott, Chairman 1950-1951

James J Bowe, Chairman 1951-1952; 1953-1954; 1955-1956; 1958-1959; 1960-1961; 1963-1964; 1967-1968; 1969-1970; 1976-1977

John O'Leary, Chairman 1952-1953

Peter Dempsey, Chairman 1954-1955

James J Kennedy, Chairman 1956-1958; 1959-1960; 1961-1962; 1965-1966

Thomas F Byrne, Chairman 1962-1963; 1966-1967; 1968-1969; 1970-1971; 1972-1973

Thaddeus J O'Loughlin, Chairman 1964-1965

Michael Darcy, Chairman 1971-1972; 1982-1983; 1993-1994

Michael Hart, Chairman 1973-1974

Andrew Doyle, Chairman 1974-1975

Seán Browne, Chairman 1975-1976

Leo Carthy, Chairman 1977-1978; 1998-1999

Thomas Howlin, Chairman 1978-1980; 1985-1986

John Roche, Chairman 1980-1982

CHAIRMEN AND VICE-CHAIRMEN 1899-1999

James Curtis, Chairman 1983-1984;
1986-1987; 1994-1995

Patrick Codd, Chairman 1984-1985

Michael Sinnott, Chairman 1987-1988

Lorcan Allen, Chairman 1988-1989;
1996-1997

Rory Murphy, Chairman 1989-1990;
1995-1996

Hugh Byrne, Chairman 1990-1991

Gus Byrne, Chairman 1991-1992

Jim Walsh, Chairman 1992-1993

John A Browne, Chairman 1997-1998

Wexford Courthouse, built in 1805, stood on the quay opposite Wexford Bridge. It was home to the county council from April 1899 until September 1920. Council meetings were held in the old grand jury room. The courthouse was destroyed by explosion and fire in the early hours of 18 June 1921 during the War of Independence. A petrol filling station now occupies the site.

Local Government in the Nineteenth Century

Wexford County Council was established one hundred years ago under the Local Government (Ireland) Act of 1898 and has been the chief instrument of local government in the county since then. Many of its functions, such as the provision of roads, bridges, housing, water-supply and sanitation, were inherited from its forerunners, the grand jury and the boards of guardians. Throughout this century, central government has devolved many other functions and responsibilities on the council, including motor taxation, driver licensing, home loans, physical planning, libraries, fire-fighting, civil defence, higher education grants, voter registration and environmental protection. To comprehend fully the council's achievements and progress since its establishment, it is necessary to examine some of the nineteenth-century administrative structures it replaced and whose functions and responsibilities it inherited.

The period 1836 to 1840 was vital to the future shape of local government in Ireland. During those years two existing elements of local government, the grand juries and the municipal towns, were significantly reformed and a third element, the boards of guardians, was introduced.

Grand Juries

Since the time of Charles I, the grand jury had been the principal body responsible for the administration of the county unit. It was composed of 'the gentlemen of most consequence in the county', namely the leading property owners. Each grand jury comprised twenty-three members who were selected by the sheriff of the county, the order in which jurors stood on the list often being an indication of their social standing. The sheriff's discretion in the nomination of the grand jury was total and, as he himself was a political appointee, he frequently filled the list with his supporters and friends.

Meetings of the grand jury were associated with the sittings of the assize courts which took place twice a year. The members met at the opening of the assize, were sworn, carried out

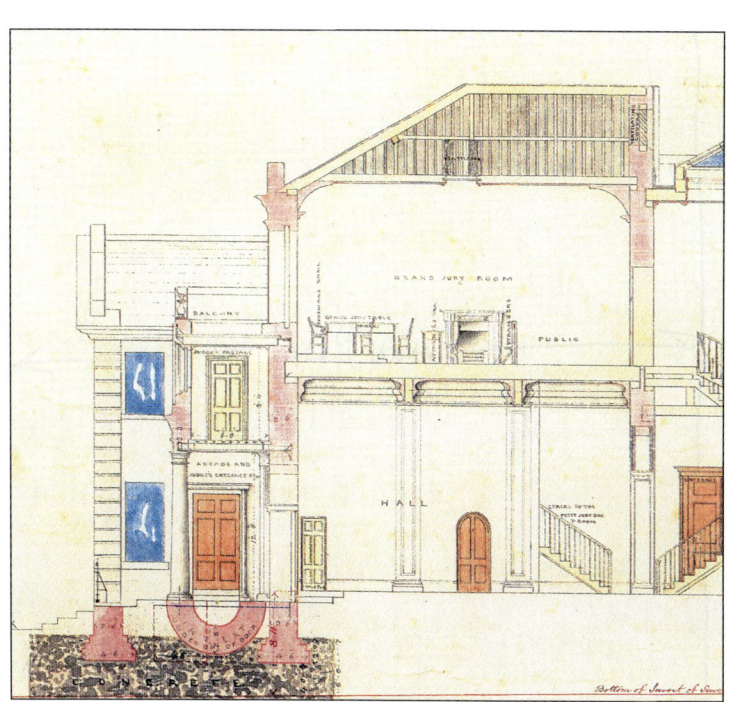

In the early 1860s, Wexford Courthouse was extensively renovated. These plans, drawn up in 1863, give details of the interior layout of the building.

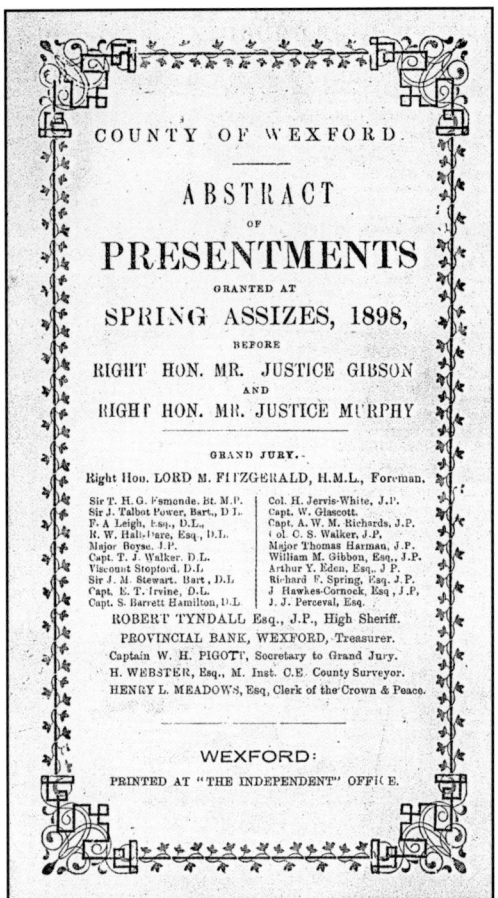

The grand jury, spring assizes 1898.

Presentments for new works at Scarawalsh given by the grand jury, spring assizes 1898.

their judicial and administrative duties and were dissolved when discharged by the judge at the end of the sessions. There was no continuity of membership unless the sheriff decided to summon the same persons for succeeding assizes. The function of the grand jury, in so far as it related to local government, was to consider and recommend to the judge of the assize the presentments recommended by the county-at-large and the baronial presentment sessions which preceded the assize. These presentment sessions consisted of a combination of justices of the peace, cess-payers listed by the grand jury of the previous session and nominees of the sheriff. There was no element of democratic election.

Presentments were, for the most part, proposals for work (e.g. the construction of a bridge or repair of a road) to be financed by levy on the baronies or the county-at-large. The work was authorised when the presentment was approved by the grand jury and the judge of assize. The cost was then levied on the property owners by means of a charge variously called grand jury cess, county cess or rates. Although there was no continuous membership of the grand jury, some employees did hold permanent positions, including the county surveyors, assistant county surveyors, secretary and treasurer, all of whom had specific statutory duties. The grand jury also owned property and was party to many contracts.

Throughout the nineteenth century, grand juries remained the preserve of the landlord class and as such never enjoyed popular support in Ireland. They were criticised for their partisanship and frequently accused of sectarianism, corruption and abuse of power. The reforming Grand Jury Act of 1836 codified their powers and responsibilities and gave cess-payers a limited role in deciding how local taxes should be spent. Until they were relieved of their administrative functions under the Local Government Act of 1898, the grand juries were responsible for making and repair of roads and bridges, the construction and maintenance of courthouses, levying rates for lunatic asylums, county infirmaries, industrial schools, coroners and certain constabulary charges.

Boards of Guardians

The Poor Relief (Ireland) Act of 1838 established the boards of guardians for 'the more effectual relief of the destitute poor in Ireland'. This Act also enabled the creation of unions in which boards of guardians administered 'relief' to the poor under the central control of the poor law commissioners. Each union comprised a number of townlands, not necessarily all within the same barony or even the same county. In all, the country was divided into 130 unions. Unlike the grand juries, the guardians included both elected and ex officio members. Justices of the peace residing in the union became ex officio guardians provided their number did not exceed one-third of the number of elective members. After 1847 the number of ex officio members could equal that of elected guardians.

Male persons of full age who were not otherwise disqualified and who were liable as occupiers for county cess in respect of a valuation of £20 (£25 in Enniscorthy Union) were eligible for election as guardians. Every person liable to pay county cess within the union was entitled to vote for the election of guardians in the electoral division in which the property was situated. Multiple votes were allowed, ranging from one vote where the valuation did not exceed £20 to six where the valuation exceeded £200. Owner-occupiers were entitled to double the

Wexford workhouse, designed to accommodate 600 inmates, was built by Wexford Board of Guardians at a cost of £6,900. Building commenced in 1840 and the house was ready for occupation in July 1842.

number of votes. Landlords were entitled to votes related to the value of the rents.

Elections were to be held every year and it was the duty of the returning officer to prepare, as the voters' list, a register of cess-payers and qualified landlords and to receive nominations for the election. Voting papers were hand-delivered to the electors who cast their votes by placing their initials opposite the names of the candidates for whom they wished to vote. They then signed the voting papers which were taken up the following day. Secrecy of the ballot was clearly not the highest priority.

The boards of guardians were closely supervised and controlled by the poor law commissioners, a body which later evolved into the Local Government Board and through further transformations into the present-day Department of the Environment. The poor law commissioners put a mass of rules and procedural orders in place to set up this detailed and comprehensive system. Separate orders were issued for each union, declaring the townlands it would comprise. Other orders specified electoral divisions and the numbers of members. In the case of the Wexford Union, for instance, the establishing order recited that it be divided into fourteen electoral divisions which were defined by reference to baronies (Forth, Bargy, Shelmaliere, Ballaghkeen and Bantry) and townlands. The electoral divisions were named as Wexford, Ardcolm, Kilpatrick, Killurin, Rathaspick, Mayglass, Rosslare, Lady's Island, Tacumshin, Kilmore, Mulrankin, Taghmon, Ambrosetown and Bannow. The number of elective guardians for the Wexford Union was twenty-four, made up of six from Wexford Electoral Division, two each from Ardcolm, Killurin, Kilmore, Mulrankin and Taghmon Electoral Divisions and one from each of the others.

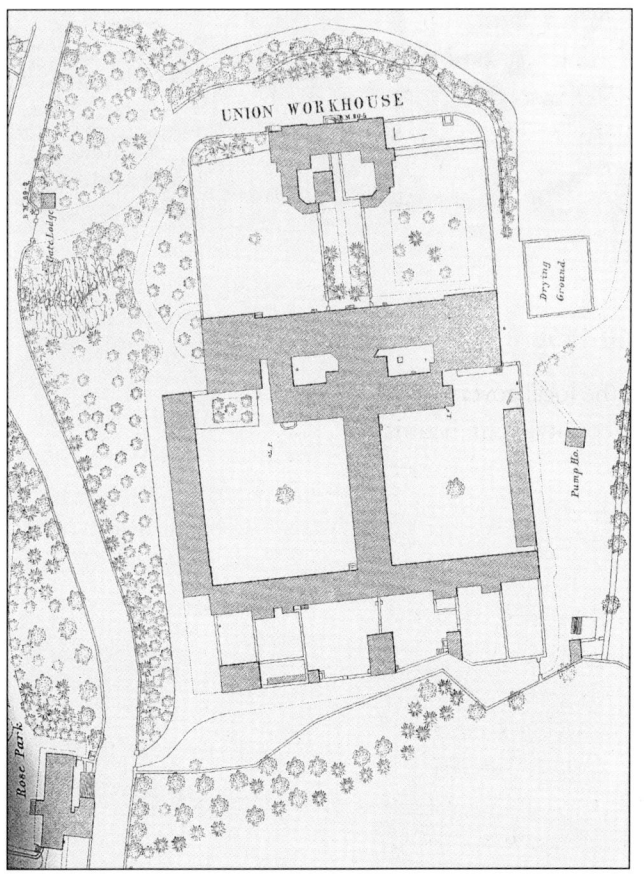

Plan of Wexford workhouse, 1883.

Similar orders were made creating the poor law unions of Enniscorthy, New Ross and Gorey, with representation as follows:

Poor Law Union	Electoral Divisions	Elected Guardians	Ex Officio Guardians
Wexford	14	24	8
Enniscorthy	14	30	10
New Ross	19*	30	10
Gorey	10	24	8

Including six in County Kilkenny and one in County Carlow

A board comprising forty, or even thirty-two, members would be considered very unwieldy today. However, that their size was not seen as a drawback can be inferred from increases in 1847 when the numbers of ex officio guardians were increased to equal the number of those elected. Likewise, in 1851 the numbers of electoral divisions were increased, resulting in even larger boards. After those increases, the strengths of the respective boards were:

Wexford	74
Enniscorthy	70
New Ross	82
Gorey	51

Municipal Towns

Many Irish towns had, over centuries, been granted royal charters establishing them as corporations of boroughs. The charters conferred a variety of duties and privileges, such as the right to hold markets, make bye-laws, hold courts, and elect members of parliament, on the inhabitants. By the year 1840 most of the corporations had become ineffectual in one way or another, resulting in the passage of the Municipal Corporations (Ireland) Act of that year. Fifty-eight of the then existing sixty-eight Irish corporations were either abolished or reduced in significance.

Four County Wexford towns were affected, namely Wexford, Enniscorthy, New Ross and Gorey. Prior to the Act they were styled

- the Mayor, bailiffs, free burgesses and commonalty of the town of Wexford
- the Portreeve, free burgesses and commonalty of the Borough of Enniscorthy
- the Sovereign and burgesses of New Ross
- the Sovereign, burgesses and free commons of the borough and town of Newborough.

In 1846 Wexford became the only Irish town to recover its former status as a municipal corporation through a new charter which was granted by Queen Victoria. The other towns became towns with commissioners under the Lighting of Towns Act or the Towns Improvement (Ireland) Act of 1854. Whether administered by commissioners or by corporations consisting of mayor, aldermen and burgesses, these communities were alike in having systems of elective town government which were organised, had recognised authority and were capable of taking on an expansion in their duties and responsibilities.

The Evolution of Local Government 1840-1898

By 1840 the disparate bodies which would later coalesce into the local government of County Wexford consisted of: the grand jury for the county; four boards of guardians; four municipal towns. These three elements were more or less independent of each other and had little in common except for the source of their funds, a cess or rate levied on local owners and occupiers of property.

The boards of guardians worked under the tight central control of the poor law commissioners. Indeed, control by the commissioners and their successors was to remain a characteristic, in varying degrees, of the developing system for very many years. The poor law commissioners and the boards of guardians set about building the workhouses with great determination and energy. By 1842 no less than eighty workhouses were either built or under construction throughout the country. Nor could the guardians rest on their oars when the buildings were in place. The orders of the commissioners were that board meetings would be held monthly until such

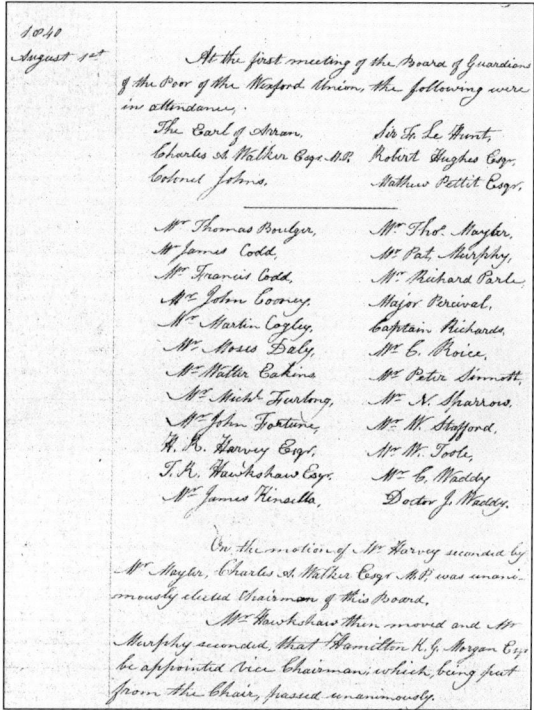

Extract from Minute book of Wexford Board of Guardians showing attendance at the board's first meeting, 1 August 1840.

time as a union workhouse was built and weekly thereafter. For many of the guardians, travelling on horseback, the round trip to the board meetings probably consumed the entire day. Given the time demanded and the discomfort of travelling in inclement weather, many guardians were probably happy that elections took place annually.

However, the guardians were very soon to face a further test, namely that of coping with the enormous rise in poverty and distress which resulted from the Great Famine. As a result of this disaster the numbers seeking admission to the workhouses came to exceed by far their design capacity. The multifarious problems of running a large institution with a resident population of several hundred men, women and children had to be resolved by a body composed of justices of the peace and property owners with little relevant previous experience. It cannot be denied that as managers the boards of guardians proved to be competent and effective bodies. They established a system and kept it operational even though at times it stretched to breaking point. They accepted the tight central control of the poor law commissioners, conscientiously corresponding with them on procedures, complying with the floods of directives, transmitting copies of their minutes, furnishing statistics and returns of their activities and assessing and collecting the poor rate.

It was not long before the government took to expanding the guardians' responsibilities. In 1851, the Medical Charities Act paved the way for a dispensary system for the sick poor. The instrument chosen by parliament to initiate this system was the poor law structure which was already in place. The boards of guardians were charged with the duties of dividing the unions into dispensary districts, electing dispensary committees comprising rate-payers and guardians, appointing officers and providing accommodation. Their responsibilities were also extended to cover the working of the dispensaries. Henceforth their meetings would include consideration of reports from the dispensary committees. Expenses under the Medical Charities Acts were included in the poor rate, which fell on the occupiers of property in the union.

Over the next forty years the guardians were assigned duties relating to parliamentary and local franchise and they became designated repositories for plans for railways and other public works. When compulsory registration of births, deaths and marriages in Ireland commenced in 1864 the guardians were made responsible for the working of the system. Superintendent registrars' and registrars' districts were established and made coterminous with the poor law unions and dispensary districts. Union employees were given first refusal of the positions of superintendent registrar and registrar. The guardians were made responsible for the custody of the registers. In 1871 an Act 'to amend and consolidate the laws relating to Juries in Ireland' placed responsibility on the clerk of the poor law union to furnish to the clerk of the peace (corresponding to the present-day county registrar) an alphabetical list of men residing in the county between the ages of twenty-one and sixty who were qualified for jury service.

Although these changes marked distinct departures from the strictly limited duties for which the boards of guardians were established in 1838, they were, nevertheless, working in a narrow framework up to 1878. In that year a fundamental expansion of the guardians' responsibilities took place with the enactment of the Public Health (Ireland) Act. Under the seemingly simple title 'An act to consolidate and amend the Acts relating to Public Health in Ireland' this enactment established a mosaic of rural and urban 'Sanitary Districts' covering the whole country. It also defined sanitary authorities and laid down their powers and duties. Municipal and town councils and commissioners left in place (or established) after the reforms of 1840 became the urban sanitary authorities. The guardians of the poor law unions became the rural sanitary authorities outside the urban areas.

Thus the guardians now found themselves with a new set of responsibilities which could be broadly described as aiming for the prevention of disease as distinct from treatment of those who had already contracted it. The objectives of the Act were to be achieved by the provision of sewers, drains, and water supplies. Scavenging of streets, control of common lodging houses, provision of burial grounds, disinfection of premises and protection against nuisances were also to come within the purview of the sanitary authorities. They were also enabled to acquire land compulsorily, borrow money and make bye-laws. Five years later the powers of rural sanitary authorities, that is the boards of guardians, were further extended by the Labourers (Ireland) Act 1883, under which the authorities could, on receiving a representation signed by not less than twelve rate-payers, make an

During the nineteenth century, responsibility for the so-called 'lunatic asylums' rested with the grand jury and the boards of guardians. After 1922 this responsibility passed to the Board of Health and Public Assistance. St Senan's Psychiatric Hospital, Enniscorthy, was the subject of extensive refurbishment and renovation programmes in the 1920s and '30s and again during the administration of Co. Manager, T F Broe.

Two-up-two-down style cottage at Rochestown, Drinagh, Wexford. Under a series of acts passed between 1883 and 1896, the boards of guardians were empowered to borrow money from the commissioners of public works to build new houses, complete with garden allotments, which were then let to labourers. The two-up-two-down labourer's cottage was the most popular style of cottage built by the guardians and their successors up to the 1930s.

improvement scheme to build houses for agricultural labourers and their families. The corresponding empowering Act for urban authorities came in 1890.

The Labourers Act incorporated the last major addition to the powers of the boards of guardians before the creation of county and rural district councils. Most of the elements which would evolve into the Irish local government system in later years had been initiated.

This, then, was the structure as the century drew to a close:

- county boroughs, boroughs and town commissioners exercising functions conferred by royal charter and statute, including the powers of urban sanitary authorities
- grand juries who were responsible for maintenance of roads and bridges, mostly by contract, and for some other public works
- boards of guardians which were established to build and operate workhouses but whose duties had been expanded to include those of rural sanitary authorities.

Funding of the services provided by these organisations was essentially by means of a rate or cess levied on property owners and occupiers. A degree of consistency in the basis for these levies had been introduced following the enactment of the Valuation (Ireland) Act 1852 under which the entire country was valued in accordance with specific criteria. The structure, however, particularly the grand juries and boards of guardians, lacked democratic input. Grand juries had no elected members and up to half the membership of the board of guardians consisted of unelected justices of the peace. Inevitably, the system resulted in boards which consisted mainly of landowners, many of whom were also landlords, who were directly affected by every change in the level of the poor rate. The boards did, however, give many people the experience of a political process on a regular basis. In addition they provided a valuable political training ground for women, who became eligible to serve as poor law guardians in 1896.

Profound social and political changes had taken place during the last three decades of the century but the intractable problems of land ownership and Home Rule continued to dominate the political consciousness of the British government and, of course, the Irish members of parliament. Governments changed but the problems persisted. The landlords' position had been weakened by the Land Acts of 1870, 1881, 1891 and 1896 and was under sustained attack from an organised tenantry. Parliamentary franchise had been broadened to include the majority of heads of households among labourers and small farmers. It was time for changes in local administration.

THE LOCAL GOVERNMENT ACT OF 1898

When the local government (Ireland) act 1898 became law on 12 August of that year it launched a package of innovations which were to have profound and lasting effects on Ireland of the twentieth century, including

- popularly elected councils for counties, rural and urban districts
- broad franchise for local authority elections
- the principle of 'one man, one vote'.

Although the Act has been extensively amended in the meantime and many of its provisions abandoned or rendered obsolete it is still the foundation stone of today's local government structure. The first section decrees that 'a council shall be established in every administrative county and be entrusted with the management of the administrative business of that county, and shall consist of a chairman and councillors'. Elsewhere it is provided that for every rural sanitary district there shall be a rural district council and, further, that all urban sanitary districts shall be called urban district councils.

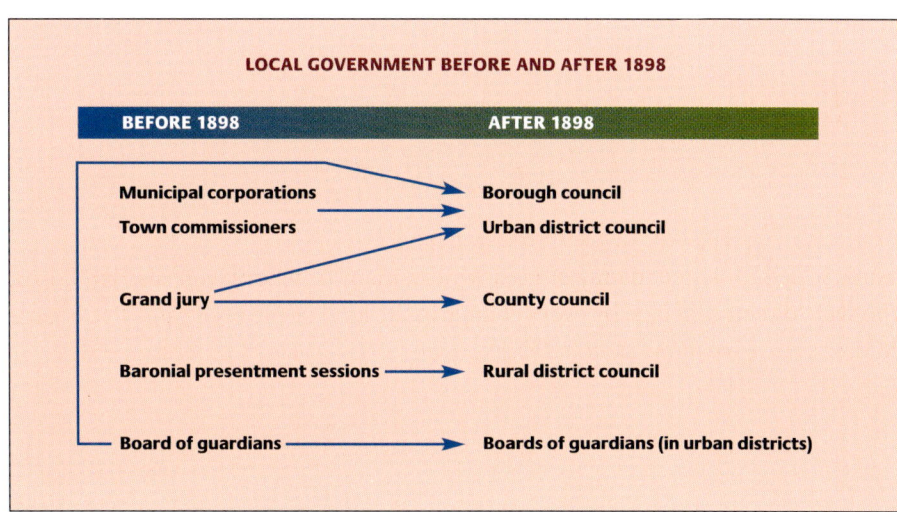

Local government before and after 1898. Reprinted, with permission of the publishers, from Virginia Crossman, LOCAL GOVERNMENT IN NINETEENTH CENTURY IRELAND, 1994, Institute of Irish Studies, Belfast.

The urban sanitary authorities in County Wexford were the Corporation of Wexford, which retained its name, and the (then) town commissioners of New Ross and Enniscorthy, each of which took the designation of urban district council. Gorey, because of its size, did not enjoy the status of an urban sanitary authority and remained part of the rural district. It continues to be a town with town commissioners. The poor law unions of Wexford, Enniscorthy and Gorey (excluding Wexford borough and Enniscorthy town), which were already rural sanitary districts under the Public Health Act, now became rural districts for which rural district councils were established under the Local Government Act.

Minor difficulties arose in the New Ross area from the facts that part of the town, the electoral division of Rosbercon Urban, was situated in County Kilkenny and the area of the New Ross Union included parts of Counties Wexford, Kilkenny and Carlow. The problems were resolved, in the case of the urban district, by altering the county boundaries to include Rosbercon Urban in County Wexford, and as regards the union, by forming three separate rural districts, each with its own rural district council, viz. the New Ross No 1 Rural District (County Wexford), the New Ross No 2 Rural District (County Kilkenny) and the New Ross No 3 Rural District (County Carlow).

The principal responsibilities of the councils were those transferred from the grand juries, the presentment sessions and the boards of guardians. They included:

County Council

- business of the county at large presentment sessions
- making and repair of roads and bridges
- construction and maintenance of courthouses
- support of lunatic asylums, county infirmaries and fever hospitals
- appointment of coroners
- levying and collecting the poor rate
- duties under the Diseases of Animals Act 1894.

Rural District Council

- business of the baronial presentment sessions
- making proposals to the county council for construction or repair of public works, e.g. roads and bridges affecting their district
- the functions of the rural sanitary authority in the district.

This transfer of responsibilities obviously had implications for the previous arrangements. The presentment sessions were abolished, the grand jury ceased to have any significance with regard to public works and the two functions of the boards of guardians with the most comprehensive impact, viz. the poor rate and the duties of rural sanitary authority, were assigned to the councils.

The boards of guardians were not, of course, abolished. They continued to be responsible for the relief of the poor, including the operation of the dispensary system, and registration of births, marriages and deaths. The old method of electing guardians and the practice of ex officio board members were ended however and the election of guardians was integrated into the new local government system. The full membership of the rural district councils became members of the boards of guardians. Special elections, associated with those for the urban district councils, were held for guardians from the urban areas. The numbers of guardians allotted to the County Wexford urban districts were:

Wexford	9
Enniscorthy	4
New Ross	8

The numerical size of the boards of guardians up to 1898 has already been given. About half the members were elected from single-seat electoral divisions, a handful from the municipal towns and up to 50% ex officio from the justices of the peace living in the union. Under the 1898 Act the electoral divisions which had been specified for the poor law unions became district electoral divisions, more or less unchanged outside the urban areas, from each of which two rural district councillors were to be elected. These councils were also empowered to co-opt three additional members at their first meeting, if they wished to do so. Obviously, the membership of the rural councils was much the same, numerically, as that of the old boards of guardians. The relevant figures in County Wexford were:

	Rural district council	Poor law guardians
Wexford	62	71
Enniscorthy	63	67
New Ross	52*	60**
Gorey	53	53

*   Refers to New Ross No 1 rural district council.
** Excludes membership from parts of Counties Kilkenny and Carlow.
    The full membership was 104.

Before 1898 the minimum qualification for election as a poor law guardian in County Wexford was to be a rate-payer in respect of a valuation of £20 (£25 in Enniscorthy Union). Rate-payers in respect of smaller valuations, although ineligible for election, were entitled to vote at the annual elections. However, multiple votes, on a scale which gave six votes each to the owner and the occupier of property valued over £200, were allowed. A person who was both owner and occupier qualified for double the number of votes. Obviously, such an electorate would produce a board with a preponderance of substantial property owners. The parliamentary franchise, on the other hand, was much broader, extending as it did to male householders, lodgers, and even occupiers of single rooms if they were let as separate tenements. The local government electors, under the new dispensation, were those entitled to the parliamentary franchise with the addition of women (if separately qualified) and peers.

The primary qualification required by candidates for election to county and district councils (and, consequently, to boards of guardians) was to be a 'local government elector'. Alternatively, twelve months' residence in the district was acceptable in the case of candidates for the district council. There were certain specific disqualifications for election, clergymen and coroners for instance. Women who were qualified as local government electors could be members of district but not of county councils. Because membership of a rural district council meant automatic membership of a board of guardians the qualifications for both of these bodies were the same.

EXEMPLAR HIBERNIAE – 100 Years of Local Government in County Wexford

THE LAST GRAND JURY FOR FISCAL PURPOSES 1899

Grand juries were relieved of their administrative functions under the Local Government Act of 1898, but retained their role in criminal proceedings. They were abolished in independent Ireland under the Criminal Justice Act of 1948, but survived at assizes in Northern Ireland until 1969.[1]

[1] SJ Connolly (ed), THE OXFORD COMPANION TO IRISH HISTORY (Oxford, 1998), p 227

SPRING ASSIZES 1899
MEMBERS OF THE GRAND JURY
SWORN BEFORE
MR FRANCIS WESTROPP DAWSON JP, CHARLESFORD, FERNS
COUNTY HIGH SHERIFF

Charles Mervyn Doyne DL, Wells (foreman)
Lord Maurice Fitzgerald HML, Johnstown Castle
Hon. Arthur Henry Chichester DL, Dunbrody Park
Robert Wesley Hall-Dare DL, Newtownbarry
Major Henry Arthur Boyse JP, Bannow House
Col. Charles Stephen Walker, The Deeps
Lord Viscount Stopford DL, Marlfield, Gorey
Capt. Samuel Barrett-Hamilton JP, Kilmannock House
John H Talbot DL, Castletalbot
Loftus Anthony Bryan DL, Borrmount Manor
Lt Col. Henry Jervis White JP, Healthfield

Albert Garner Richards JP, Macmine Castle
Robert Tyndall JP, Oaklands
Capt. Arthur William Mordaunt Richards JP, Ardamine
Joseph E Deane-Drake JP, Stokestown
Arthur Henry Tyndall JP, Ballyanne
Arthur Yelverton Eden JP, Merton
Richard F Spring JP, Polehore
William Monk Gibbon JP, Templesheelin
Frederick Hughes, Barntown
J Hawkes-Cornock JP, Cromwellsfort
John J Perceval, Barntown,
James E Stannard, Bricketstown

EMPLOYEES OF THE GRAND JURY AT SPRING ASSIZES 1899

List compiled from salaries presented at the grand jury session

Capt. W H Piggott, Secretary
Thomas Wilkinson, Sub-Sheriff
Henry Webster, County Surveyor
William Ryan, County Surveyor's Assistant
Mr W H Jones, County Surveyor's Assistant
Patrick Leary, County Surveyor's Assistant
James P Murphy, County Surveyor's Assistant
Dr J R Cardiff, Coroner
Dr Denis P Murphy, Coroner
Salary of Surgeon to county infirmary also presented although not an officer of the grand jury
David Haddon Esq., Surgeon to the county infirmary

The Elections of 1899

THE FIRST ELECTIONS under the 1898 Act were to the municipal bodies – corporations of boroughs, urban district councils and town commissioners – and were held on 16 January 1899. They passed off reasonably quietly in County Wexford, probably because there was already a tradition of elective authorities in the towns. The main difference this time lay in the extended electorate. The extent of this change can be appreciated from the Wexford Borough figures where the number entitled to vote increased from 217 to 2,179, including 194 women.

Whether the wider franchise affected the outcome of these elections is a matter for debate. The entire body of outgoing commissioners was returned in Gorey. Of the seventeen outgoing members seeking re-election to Wexford Corporation, fourteen were successful, leaving eleven newcomers on the municipal council. In Enniscorthy, where the new council comprised fifteen members, it was reported that 'the change practically amounts to a revolution in the municipal body, the

Late nineteenth-century Wexford town.

infusion of new blood making nearly half the board'. The announcement of the results in New Ross, where three merchants were elected for the Rosbercon urban division and twelve Labour or Nationalist candidates for the New Ross urban division, 'was greeted with jubilation by a large crowd who waited outside the Tholsel until a late hour'.

If the municipal elections passed off quietly, apart from the celebrations and congratulations attending the results, it was a different story in the rural areas. The county and rural district council elections were innovative in a constituency that had previously been devoid of any official outlet for the political hopes, aspirations and feelings of a large part of the electorate. Moreover, there were many contentious and topical issues exercising the minds of the new electorate. The rural elections were scheduled for 6 April, which gave more time to candidates and their supporters to prepare their campaigns and there was no shortage of candidates to take up the cudgels.

The flow of paper from the Local Government Board in Dublin from autumn 1898 to spring 1899 included several circulars to the boards of guardians about the coming changes in their status and duties, not least directions for handing over responsibilities and, where relevant, bank balances, to the new organisations. The guardians were also consulted about proposed boundary changes, transfer of staff, contracts and a myriad of other details. It was probably inevitable that the benefits of a common approach from the entire county would be raised and, indeed, Mr C H Peacocke suggested, at the meeting of the Wexford Guardians in November 1898, a convention of delegates from the 'representative' bodies in the county to formulate a course of action in anticipation of the forthcoming elections. After some debate as to whether 'representative' was synonymous with 'elective' a meeting was organised for 4 January 1899, and was attended by members of the four boards of guardians, the Enniscorthy and Gorey Town Commissioners and the Wexford Corporation.

This meeting passed resolutions suggesting that local meetings be held to select candidates to go forward in the 124 district electoral divisions for election to the rural district councils and in the eighteen county electoral divisions for election to the county council. However, it became obvious during the course of this meeting that the delegates were aware of another, and for some at least, more significant, convention which was to take place shortly.

A fund with the interesting name of the 'Pay the Members and Evicted Tenants Fund' had existed in the county for some years. It was managed by a standing committee under the chairmanship, in 1898, of Rev. P Kenny PP, Oulart, with Rev. Patrick Doyle, Camolin, and Mr J M Walsh as joint honorary secretaries. The standing committee summoned a county convention annually to review the results of parish collections for the fund and to approve the payment of subventions to a small number of tenant farmers who had been evicted because of their refusal or inability to pay rent. The fund also made payments to MPs for the county who, at that time, were not paid as parliamentarians.

On 24 December 1898, the joint secretaries gave notice that the 1899 annual convention would take place in the Assembly Rooms, Wexford, on Monday 31 January 1899. Four delegates were invited from each parish or district and clergy were ex officio members. This meeting was variously called the 'County Convention' and the 'Nationalist Convention'. However, it was the final paragraph of the advertisement which attracted the most attention and persuaded the guardians and commissioners attending the meeting on 4 January that greater things would happen at the Nationalist Convention. It promised that

> as matters of the very gravest importance will be under consideration which are of interest to Irish Nationalists of every shade of opinion, particularly the policy to be pursued in the selection of candidates for the County and District Councils, and probably the making of arrangements for the calling of district meetings to select suitable candidates, cards will be forwarded to a number of representative gentlemen who of late years have differed in some respects from the policy of the County Wexford Convention.

Father Doyle also wrote a letter to the *Free Press* which was published on 11 January explaining that the selection of an early date for the 1899 convention resulted from

> a pretty general demand from the Local Government electors of the County for the Convention to be held at such a date as would enable light and leading to be given regarding the method of choosing candidates for the County and District Councils and regarding the general purposes of the very complicated and important Local Government Act.

The convention was comprehensively reported in the *Free Press* of 4 February and the names of the 170 delegates were faithfully listed. After the routine business of the meeting was concluded the delegates got down to considering the other items on the agenda. It was obviously these matters, together with the earlier call to 'Irish Nationalists of every shade of opinion' which attracted the large attendance. Resolutions were passed relating to many of the burning issues of the day: the right of Irishmen to legislate for their own people; the financial grievances of over-taxation of Ireland; the demands for fair play in education, particularly in relation to a Catholic University; and demands for changes in the Land Acts. The convention went on to welcome the Local Government Act as a measure that would 'speedily lead on to the goal of legislative independence'. However, it recommended care in the selection of candidates for the forthcoming county and rural district councils and suggested that only men 'whose aspirations reflected the views of the majority of Irish people and were practical and sensible representatives of all classes and creeds' should be put forward.

Mr T J Healy MP and Mr Peter Ffrench MP addressed the convention. In relation to the Local Government Act, Mr Healy argued strongly in favour of including some Unionists on the councils:

> … we have to ask ourselves if, on the one hand, we are to adopt the advice given by some prominent Irishmen that we are to elect nobody to those County or Rural District Councils except Home Rulers, or, on the other hand, are we to say [that] some of those

gentlemen go with us on nearly every other subject except Home Rule.

Mr Healy went on to impress upon his audience that there was more at stake than what went on at local level.

> We will be on our trial as to our capacity to work the Local Government Act, not for the benefit of any one class, but for the benefit of all Ireland. I believe in making the County Councils and District Councils overwhelmingly National, but, subject to that, I am in favour of giving Unionists fair representation on those bodies.
>
> The reason I am in favour of their admission is this – I have always consistently condemned the actions of the Grand Juries in their exclusive policy and I am not now going to practice a policy I have always condemned in others.
>
> Another reason is this – during the passage of Mr Gladstone's Home Rule Bill, the strongest argument that was always used against us was that, if the Home Rule Bill was passed, Unionists would find it impossible to live in Ireland. I want to take the strongest argument away from the anti-Home Rulers. I want to point to the action of the County Councils and say, 'Here you have Unionists elected, now what have you to be afraid of ?'

With regard to the selection of candidates for the forthcoming elections, the convention decided, after considerable debate, that

> the clergy of each Electoral Division, with the Poor Law Guardians attending the Meeting here today, be appointed to call together the District voters for the selection of candidates for the District Council and that two delegates for each Electoral Division be appointed to attend a further meeting to select candidates for the (County) Electoral Area.

The request to the clergy and poor law guardians was enthusiastically fulfilled. Over the succeeding weeks the *Free Press* reported on selection meetings in at least sixty-seven venues throughout the county. It was expected that by giving the electors the opportunity of nominating candidates at local meetings those selected would have enough community support to ensure their subsequent election. It was also hoped that, as the candidates were chosen in their own districts and by their neighbours and acquaintances, many of them would be unopposed.

The new councils were supposed to be non-political bodies and, indeed, they seem to have met that criterion in their performance and work. However, it is obvious that strong political feelings and hopes underlay the process of selecting candidates. Speakers at the local meetings, particularly the selected candidates, repeatedly referred to the topics of Home Rule, education, taxation, tenants' rights, and working conditions. At some meetings there was outspoken opposition to Unionists and members of the grand jury. Candidates were regularly identified by their political affiliation – Nationalist, Labour, Irish Party supporters etc.

The local meetings succeeded in their objective of identifying candidates capable of commanding local support. Consequently, more than eighty of the seats on the rural district councils and several on the county council were uncontested. Indeed, a note of criticism could be detected later against candidates who had insisted on going forward without preliminary local endorsement and had thereby been responsible for the expense of a contested election falling on the rate-payers. A more sustainable criticism was advanced in a *Free Press* editorial on 11 March 1899 in which the selection procedure through local meetings was described as the 'great caucus scheme which was to enforce practical unanimity' but which had, in some cases, caused bitter division between aspirants and forced neighbours to take sides openly.

The local press, in addition to comprehensive coverage, did not hesitate to comment and advise. On the eve of the municipal elections on 14 January 1899 the *Free Press* remarked, 'Today we may fairly say the brake has been taken off and the coach of democracy let progress at full speed'. As the date for the county and rural district council elections approached editorial comments became more frequent and directive. From mid-February to election-day almost every week's editorial was on the subject of the elections. They strongly favoured Nationalist and Catholic candidates and warned their readers against supporting Unionists and former members of the grand jury.

A week after the elections the *Free Press* editorial gave its verdict: 'Ireland is thus today – as far as local government goes – in the possession of her own people'. It went on to support the suggestion in the following letter from Sir Thomas H G Esmonde MP, and now member of the county council, which it published under the title 'A People's Parliament':

> The first resolution to be adopted by the Irish County Councils at their Meeting on April 22nd will be, I take it, one asserting our right of legislative independence.
>
> Following that resolution, I would venture to suggest another, conceived to give it practical effect. With this object I hope to have the honour of proposing, for the acceptance of Wexford County Council, that two members of the Council be delegated to meet, upon a date to be subsequently fixed by mutual consent in Dublin, two delegates from as many of the other County Councils in Ireland as see fit to assent to the suggestion, for the purpose of considering such public matters as may be deemed worthy of their attention and of taking such action in relation to them as may be deemed useful in the National interest.
>
> If the suggestion be generally adopted, we would have at once a 'People's Parliament', the first since 1641.

This issue also printed a letter under the title 'The Toleration Tommyrot' from Michael Davitt, founder of the Land League, vehemently asserting that, having fought so long and hard to overcome the power and influence of the landlords, it would be utterly illogical now to restore any vestige of their power by electing them to the new councils. This was obviously aimed at the prevalent idea that, as suggested by T J Healy MP on 31 January 1899, the councils would use their discretionary powers to co-opt one or more Unionists at their first meeting.

The final words on the impact and expectations flowing from the new arrangements are left to Judge Andrews in his address to the grand jury at the start of the summer assizes 1899:

> Since this time last year, when it was my duty to address the Grand Jury of the County of Wexford, a vast change has been effected by Parliament over the whole County – over the whole country of Ireland – in the duties of Grand Jurors. They have now been transferred to the County and District Councils and it means the laying of the foundation stone of the liberties of a free people – that those who pay the taxes should, through their elected representatives, impose and disburse those taxes.

The majority of the new councillors may not have been totally satisfied that they had yet reached the status of a 'free people' but they did go about their responsibilities seriously. Collectively, they were a much different group from the grand jury and the boards of guardians but, nonetheless, the break from the old order was not absolute. Three members of the first council who came through the electoral process had served as grand jurors in the previous year: John Cummins, Shielbaggin, James A Doyle, Templesheelin, and Laurence Murphy, Ballykerogue. Because membership of the grand jury was not continuous, the members being discharged by the judge at the close of the assize sittings, it is possible that other councillors had also served on it in earlier years.

In addition, the grand jury selected for the spring assizes of 1899 was given the facility of nominating three members to the first county council from those who had served as grand jurors in the previous three years. Those chosen were Charles M Doyne, Wells, Gorey, Lord Viscount Stopford, Marlfield, Gorey, and Capt. Thomas J Walker, Tykillen, Kyle, Wexford. The county council itself was also empowered, as its first act, to co-opt two additional members. In the event, the two selected, Captain Loftus A Bryan of Borrmount and Lord Maurice Fitzgerald, Johnstown Castle, had also served as grand jurors in the previous year. Thus eight of the twenty-eight councillors had served as grand jurors. Several former poor law guardians also became members of the county council and even more took places on the rural district councils. Consequently, although the structures were changed fundamentally, a perceptible link remained between the new and the old.

The First Meeting of the Council

ON 22 APRIL 1899 the newly-elected councillors, together with the representatives of the rural district councils, met for the first time in the grand jury room at Wexford courthouse. They quickly got down to the formal business of co-opting additional councillors and the election of the chairman and vice-chairman. Mr James Donohue JP, Templeshannon, Enniscorthy, was

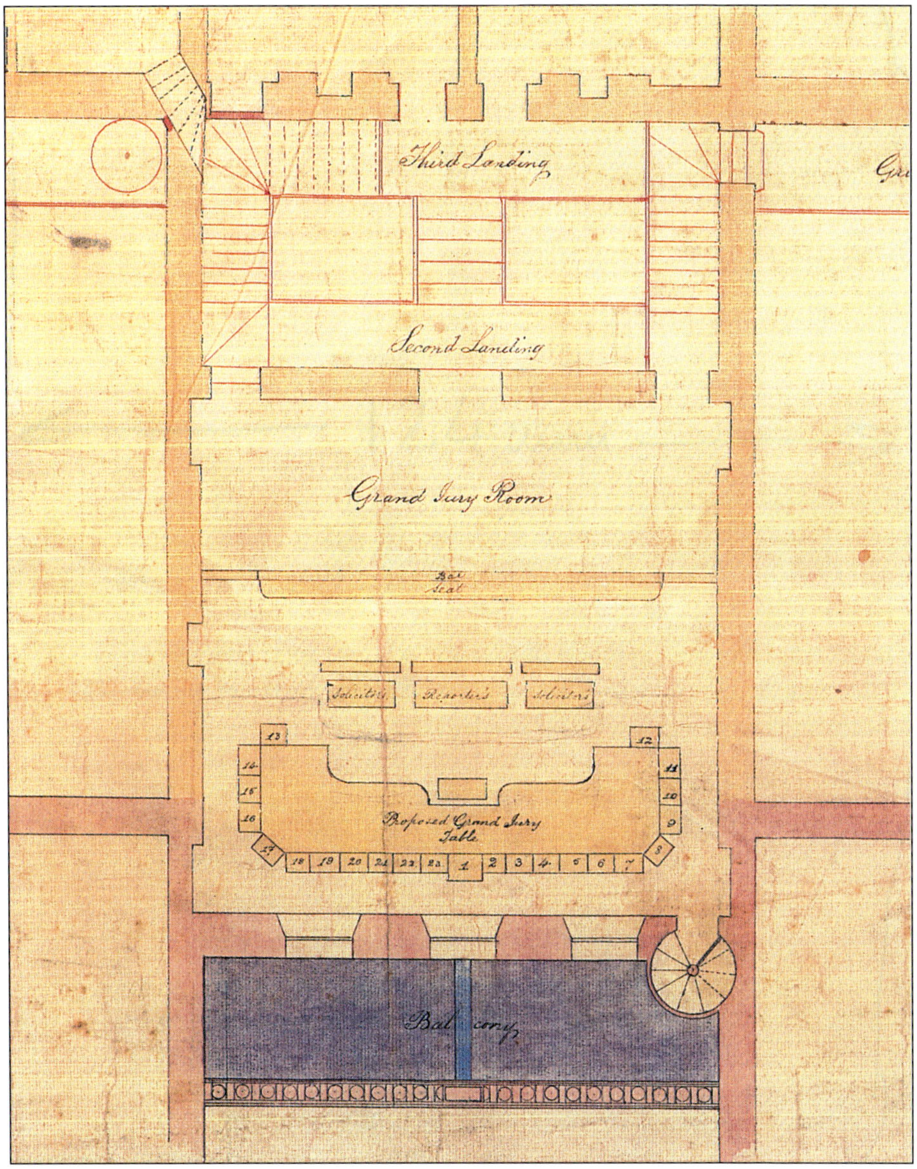

Layout of grand jury room, Wexford Courthouse, where Wexford County Council met for the first time on 22 April 1899.

Sir Thomas Henry Grattan Esmonde was the eldest son of Sir John Esmonde, MP and Louise Grattan, granddaughter of Henry Grattan. He was born at Pau in France and educated at St Mary's Roman Catholic College at Oscott in Staffordshire. From 1885 to 1891 he served as Irish National Party MP for South Dublin and was subsequently MP for West Kerry, 1891-1900. In 1898 he became Papal Chamberlain Knight Grand Commander in Ireland of the Order of the Holy Sepulchre. Sir Thomas was an ardent nationalist and a strong supporter of John Redmond's Irish Parliamentary Party in its struggle for Home Rule. He was MP for North Wexford from 1900 until 1918.

On 22 April 1899 he was elected chairman of Wexford County Council, a position he held until 1909. In December 1899 he presented the council with its official seal. He served on the council until 1911 and was also chairman of the Gorey Board of Guardians (1898-1918) and of Arklow Harbour Board (1900-1915). Sir Thomas was a strong advocate of the preservation of Ireland's archaeological heritage and ancient placenames and was a member of both the Royal Society of Antiquaries and the Royal Dublin Society. He wrote several well-received books including *Hunting Memories of Many Lands* (1925) and *More Hunting Memories* (1930). He also contributed articles to *The Field* and to the *Newfoundland Quarterly*.

Sir Thomas was returned to the Senate of the Irish Free State in 1922 as an independent. In March 1923, while attending a meeting in London, he received word that his family home at Ballynestragh, near Gorey, had been burned by anti-Treaty forces. All family and other historical documents together with a very extensive library were completely destroyed. Sir Thomas continued as senator until 1934. He died in 1935, a year before the reconstruction of Ballynestragh was completed.

List of those attending the first meeting of Wexford County Council, 22 April 1899.

County Council Minute book, 22 April 1899, records Sir Thomas Grattan Esmonde's proposal for a council of county councillors to meet to discuss matters of mutual interest. His proposal led to the eventual formation of the General Council of County Councils.

elected to preside pending the election of a chairman.

There was just one nominee for chairman, Sir Thomas Henry Grattan Esmonde, who was declared elected. Sir Thomas took the chair and asked for nominations for the office of vice-chairman. Again, there was only one name put forward and Mr Edmond Hore of Coldblow, Broadway, was deemed elected. After disposing of the mandatory business, the council turned to some of the topics which had been preeminent during the months before the elections and the members recorded resolutions which clearly demonstrated the collective aspirations for Ireland's future.

The first three resolutions passed by Wexford County Council, 22 April 1899.

On the proposal of Mr Donohue, seconded by Mr O Doyle it was resolved:

> That the people of Ireland are a free people with a natural right to govern themselves, that no Parliament is competent to make laws for Ireland except an Irish Parliament sitting in Ireland and that we repudiate the claim of any other legislature or government to legislate for or govern the people of this country.

A further proposal of Mr Ryan, seconded by Mr Maylor, 'that we protest against the continued over-taxation of Ireland and call on our representatives in Parliament to insist on immediate steps being taken by the Government to afford us restitution', was also passed. The motion proposed by Mr Hearne and seconded by Mr Codd, 'that we assert the right of the Irish people to justice in the matter of higher education and call on the Government to take the necessary measures for the establishment and fitting endowment of a Catholic University for Ireland', met with unanimous approval.

Recognising, perhaps, that these laudable hopes could only be realised with the will of the government, the council then turned to a matter which was within its own control and had been foreshadowed by Sir Thomas H G Esmonde's letter published in the previous week's paper. The newly-elected chairman proposed the following motion which was seconded by Mr Hearne and passed:

> That we appoint a delegation of three members of this Council to meet in Dublin a similar delegation from each of the other Irish County Councils and from each of the six County Borough Councils in Ireland for the purpose of discussing from time to time such matters of public interest and of taking such action upon them as may be deemed advisable.

This resolution was, as we shall see, to have a lasting result which the newly established council could hardly have expected but which survives even to the present. However, the council then returned to more mundane issues. The councillors decided: to appoint the National Bank Ltd as their treasurer; to appoint a finance committee of seven members; to appoint a standing orders committee; and that the statutory proposals committee would comprise the entire council. They also decided that twelve members would be elected to the Enniscorthy District Lunatic Asylum Committee of Management and that Most Rev. Dr Browne, Ven. Arch-Deacon Latham, Rev. J Dunne Adm. and Mr J Cullen JP would be appointed to the same committee. As a result of the addition of the Rosbercon Urban District Electoral Division to County Wexford the bridge at New Ross no longer marked the boundary between counties Kilkenny and Wexford. The councillors therefore proposed that the Local Government Board be asked to leave the cost of maintaining New Ross bridge, as heretofore, to be shared equally with Kilkenny County Council. The members of the first finance committee, of whom three would form a quorum, were: Sir Thomas Esmonde, Lord Viscount Stopford, J F Walsh, C H Peacocke, J B Hearne, P Ryan and C M Doyne.

This ended the proceedings of this historic meeting which was to a large extent concerned with setting the scene for future business. The cordial atmosphere in which the work had been done augured well for co-operation and harmony in the future.

Founding of the General Council of County Councils

As already mentioned, the county council resolved on 22 April 1899 to propose a meeting in Dublin of delegates from all county councils for periodic discussion and action on matters of common interest. In fact, county borough councils were similarly invited to participate. In May Sir Thomas Esmonde wrote to the other council chairmen asking that resolutions similar to that already passed in Wexford in support of a national convention be adopted in all areas. In addition to strong support from the *Free Press*, which published an editorial on 27 May under the title 'The All-Ireland Council', the *Irish Daily Independent* reported in June under the heading 'The People's Parliament' that 'a sufficient number of County Councils has now approved of Sir Thomas Esmonde's suggestion for a central congress in Dublin to warrant the belief that it can have practical results'.

The *Wexford Independent* of 23 August 1899 praised the 'Conference of the Chairmen of County Councils' which, it reported,

> was held in the Ancient Concert Rooms, Dublin, on yesterday, Tuesday, under the presidency of the originator of the idea, Sir Thomas Esmonde. Delegates from over twenty counties, representative of all parties attended and the beneficial results that will accrue from their consultation will, no doubt, be many and far-reaching.

The *Irish Times* was also enthusiastic:

> We can see great value in a General Council which will assist the County Councils in keeping to business and in discharging it in a rapid, adequate and successful manner. The names that we elsewhere give of the Chairmen who are expected to meet on the forthcoming occasion are of gentlemen fully acquainted with the affairs of Counties and qualified to treat them in all respects authoritatively. From the deliberations of such experienced persons we can confidently expect that the best conclusions will result. We should hope that the movement will exactly supply what is required in training Councillors in their responsibilities and duties. Everyone will agree with us that Sir Thomas Esmonde deserves the highest credit for his energy and perseverance in bringing this organised effort to render the working of the Councils easier so far on the way to the success which we can venture to expect for it.

The next edition of the *Wexford Independent* included an extensive report of the meeting during which Sir Thomas Esmonde was elected chairman and spoke at some length on his hopes and ambitions for the general council. By the time the second meeting took place on 3 December, the name The General Council of the Irish County Councils had evolved and it is under this title, or a near variant, that the organisation has continued as the recognised body and collective voice of county councils up to the present.

THE SEAL OF WEXFORD COUNTY COUNCIL

The seal was presented to the council by Sir Thomas H Grattan Esmonde at its meeting of 11 December 1899. In his presentation speech, Sir Thomas described the seal as an 'exceedingly handsome specimen of engraving', and said that it reflected great credit on its Irish craftsmen. He expressed the hope that it would 'always seal the records of the business capacity and financial prosperity of Wexford County Council'.

The seal is divided into four, each part representing one of the principal towns of the county; Wexford, Enniscorthy, New Ross and Gorey. The harp in the centre of the seal symbolises either Ireland or the province of Leinster.

Wexford (top left) is represented by the seal of its mayor and corporation.

Enniscorthy (bottom left) is represented by the town's coat of arms which is described as follows: 'Azure, on a mount vert, a castle or, and from the battlements an eagle issuant argent'.

New Ross (top right): 'On a bridge of five arches over water, a stag and greyhound in full course towards the sinister, the dog with its head regardent biting at the neck of the stag'. Only three of the five arches referred to in the town's coat of arms appear in its representation on the council seal.

Gorey (bottom right): On 24 November 1623, the town received its first coat of arms which has four pictorial representations; a cross, a swan with eel in its beak, a lion and a rose. These figures are symbolic of religion, industry, fortitude, and unanimity.

The seal is still used to authenticate council documents.

One Hundred Years of Local Government – A Manager's Perspective

SEAMUS DOOLEY, WEXFORD COUNTY MANAGER

ON BEING ASKED TO WRITE this article reflecting on our centenary from an executive perspective it appeared at first to be a straightforward task. In practice, trying to encapsulate one hundred years of local government in a meaningful way for modern readers proved very daunting. Almost no trace of the society which created the local government system now remains. At the time the council was established in 1899 Ireland was under British rule and we were largely an agrarian and traditional society. We have moved from there through independence to our present position as an urban, largely industrial society with citizens possessed of an increasingly European and international outlook. Local government has been hugely influential in facilitating these changes and in creating the society we have today. In reaching an appreciation and understanding of the pivotal role of local government in our community we need to consider some of the major events and trends which have influenced our development.

Origins of the Council

At the end of the nineteenth century the arrangements in place for the local administration of government policy can only be described as unsatisfactory. Because Ireland was under British rule at that time all major policy decisions were made in London and administration at local level was in the hands of a plethora of local bodies acting independently of each other. In general terms these bodies were representative of the establishment and the general body of the citizens was excluded from the decision-making process. In England a similar situation had been addressed by the Local Government Act 1888 which transferred most local functions to county councils. However, in Ireland reform was delayed. This was principally due to unionist fears of nationalist domination of the new bodies. By 1898 these issues had been resolved and the Local Government (Ireland) Act 1898 created our present local government structures with democratically elected councils responsible for a range of local functions and the local administration of government policy The Act also provided that:

> All urban sanitary authorities ... shall be called urban district councils and their districts shall be called urban districts [1]

Local elections to Wexford County Council were held on the 6 April 1899 and the franchise was extended to householders, which included women for the first time.

Seán (John R) Etchingham was born at Ballintray, Courtown, in 1870. A journalist by profession, he became actively involved in the Irish Volunteers and was one of the leaders of the 1916 Rising in Enniscorthy. He was elected to Dáil Éireann in 1918 and was Minister of Fisheries from 1920 until 1922. In 1920 and again in 1922 he was elected chairman of Wexford County Council but, due to the political situation, his attendance was infrequent. He died at his home in Courtown on 23 April 1923. On 12 September 1944, Eamonn de Valera unveiled a memorial to Seán Etchingham at Ardamine.

John J O'Byrne, Cushenstown, New Ross was elected interim chairman of Wexford County Council in 1921, 'until Mr J R Etchingham would be available'. He first became a member of the county council on 12 November 1915 when he was co-opted to replace a Mr R A Rice and was subsequently elected in the 1920 local elections. The events of the civil war saddened him and he could not be persuaded to contest the 1925 election. He died unexpectedly on 18 October 1929.

The first meeting of Wexford County Council was held on 22 April 1899 when Sir Thomas Esmonde was elected chairman. The meeting went on to pass resolutions declaring the right of self-government for the Irish people and demanding changes to the Land Act, which perhaps illustrates that the fears of unionists about the new structures were well founded. It is difficult for today's observer to appreciate the significance of the creation of the county councils. In these times we take the rights of our citizens and our system of local government for granted. However in 1899 these events had enormous significance and were hugely influential in the evolution of political events in Ireland in the twentieth century. It has been written of the 1898 legislation:

> It worked a social revolution; it completely disestablished the ascendancy class from its position of power and made the mass of Irish people masters of all the financial and local affairs of Ireland.[2]

These developments ended the domination of the landlord class in Irish local government and were a precursor to the move to full independence.

> In its own way, this was as far-reaching a transfer of power as the Treaty was to bring; and indeed the adherence of county councils to the Republican cause was to do a great deal to make the Treaty attainable.[3]

At a time when there was no national forum for nationalist sentiments it was perhaps inevitable that the divisions in society on the *national* question would be reflected in the council chamber. The local government system in the main backed the nationalist cause and transferred allegiance to the first Dáil when it was created in 1919. These were difficult times and on several occasions during the War of Independence the offices of Wexford County Council were ransacked and the county secretary and acting chairman of the council were arrested. However despite these intrusions the work of the council was maintained.

Building a New State

Following independence the attention of the new Irish government turned to developing Ireland's infrastructure, which lagged significantly behind international standards at that time. Local authorities played a central role in that reconstruction and for many decades the construction and operation of infrastructure such as piped water, sewers, and roads constituted the primary activity of the local government system.

At the time of the creation of county councils roads were rural in character and were mainly for horse-drawn transportation. The railway system carried the bulk of long-distance traffic and the road network was mainly for local use. In Wexford for instance, none of the public roads had a tarmacadam surface and all of the bridges were entirely or partly made of timber. The urban areas were generally supplied with water and sewers but outside towns these services were almost non-existent. By 1946 only 8.6% of rural dwellers in Ireland had piped water compared with 92% in towns.

In the early years of the century, most rural roads were little more than dirt tracks. They required almost constant maintenance and were the subject of much criticism especially by owners of motor vehicles who advocated the use of steam rollers on roads to improve their surface.

In the late 1920s and early '30s the council began to use concrete as a road surface. Picture shows stretch of Enniscorthy concrete road still extant in May 1970.

With substantial state support an investment programme of improvement to infrastructure was undertaken. Beginning in the 1920s priority in road improvement was given to developing routes of national importance between towns. This work was greatly accelerated by Ireland's entry into the European Economic Community in 1973. Access to funding under the European Regional Development Fund (structural funds) and later the Cohesion Fund allowed the development of Irish roads to progress at a faster rate than would have been possible from our own

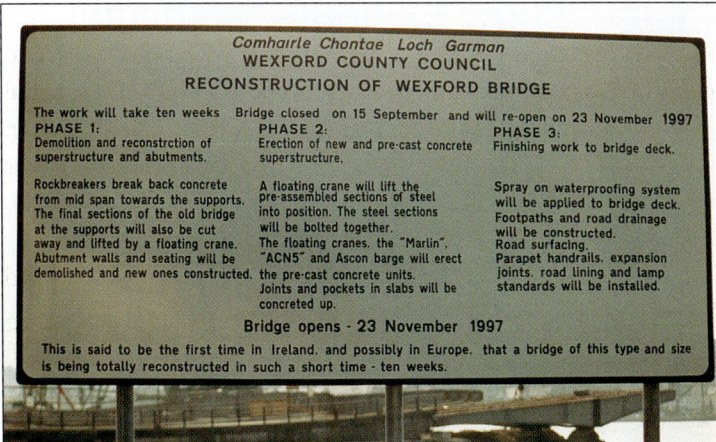

Information board at site of reconstruction of Wexford Bridge, September to November 1997.

The Automobile Association provided road signs in the county for many years. This one at Clonegal was photographed in January 1975.

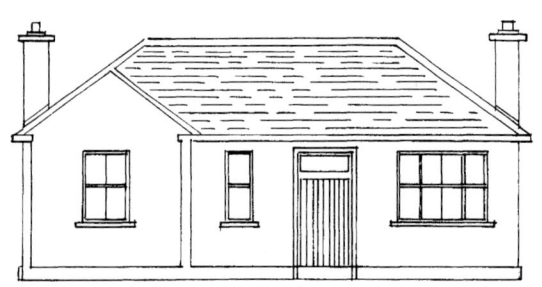

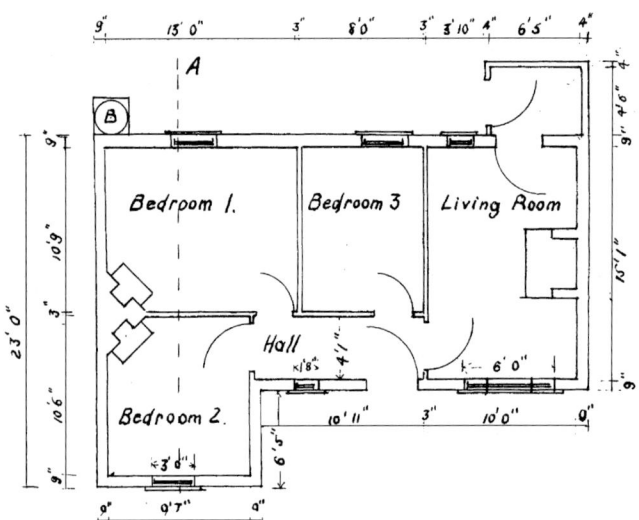
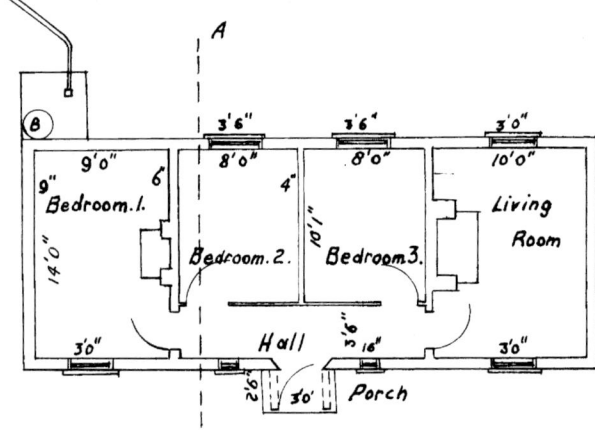
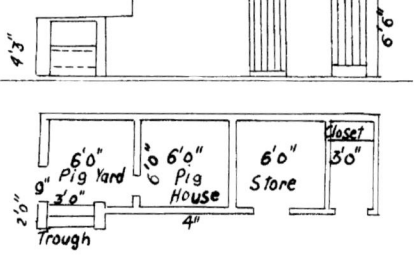

Cottages of the type built prior to 1942 by the Board of Health and Public Assistance. Each cottage had an adjacent outhouse containing a dry toilet and a pig house with an adjoining pig yard. This single story cottage type replaced the traditional two-up-two-down labourer's cottage.

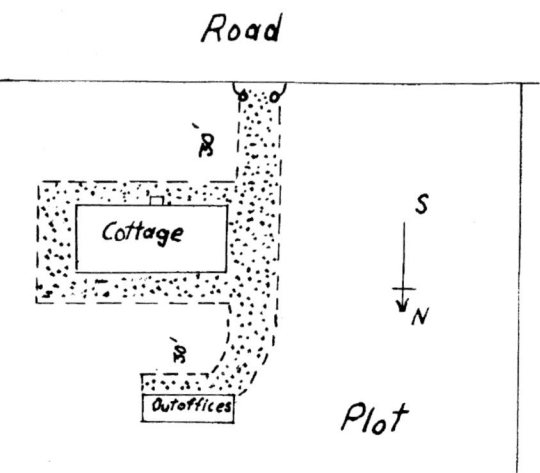

resources. Wexford has benefited substantially from the investment programme particularly on the N11 from Dublin to Wexford, the N30 from Enniscorthy to New Ross and the N25 from Cork to Rosslare. The reconstruction of Wexford Bridge in 1997 was also assisted from EU funds.

The development of rural water and sewerage services dates primarily from the 1950s and 1960s. By that time the lack of adequate services was seen as a bar to economic development and as an essential social need. In 1959 a programme to develop rural services was begun. Wexford was an early beneficiary with a grant of £100,000 allocated towards the regional water supply scheme in south Wexford. The development of water and sewage services has also benefited from funding from the European Union. The EU has been very influential in setting standards for drinking water and for disposal of sewage effluent. Most of our current practices in this area are governed by EU directives. Today in Ireland over 700,000 households are supplied with piped water by their local authorities and the construction of modern plant ensures that we will continue to supply our customers with services to the best international standards.

Although much has been achieved in the provision of infrastructure, much remains to be done. Changing demographic patterns and the growing economy will continue to place a strain on our roads and sanitary services. Wexford County Council estimates that investment of £130 million on national routes and £103 million on water and sewerage infrastructure will be required over the next five years to meet the needs in these areas in County Wexford. This investment is essential to our future and Wexford County Council looks forward to assisting in the investment programme.

Social Housing

Since the establishment of county councils the provision of public housing has always been one of the most important of our operations. It is often the service most visible and identified by the public as a local government function. The provision of adequate housing for all citizens has been a priority of the state since its inception and local government has been the channel through which most of this housing has been provided. We can be proud of our record and there is no doubt that local authorities have made an immeasurable improvement to the lives of thousands ofour citizens through our public housing programmes.

At the time of the establishment of county councils most Irish people lived in terrible conditions, often in one-room, mud-walled cabins with thatched roofs in rural areas and in appalling slum conditions in towns. Although some progress was made in the early part of the century the housing situation remained the most urgent social problem facing the new

Single storey council cottage at Grageen, Mayglass.

County council village scheme at Clonroche.

Each year Wexford County Council builds over one hundred houses.

government in 1922. They immediately launched a programme to build local authority houses and this work was continued by Irish governments ever since.

Local government proved well able for the challenge and between 1923 and 1964 over 73,000 local authority houses were built. The Housing Act (1966) replaced more than fifty earlier housing acts and its provisions are still the primary source of the local authority's powers and functions relating to housing today.

The provision of housing by local authorities continues and each year Wexford County Council builds over one hundred houses. However it is recognised that our housing needs cannot be fully met by the provision of public housing alone. In 1991 the government set out its policy in *A Plan for Social Housing* and this policy was extended and updated in 1995 with the document *Social Housing – The Way Ahead*. These plans strengthen the council's role in the housing function but the emphasis is on the facilitation of housing provision as distinct from the direct provision of housing. The programmes contain a number of innovative measures including shared ownership schemes, repairs to private housing in lieu of rehousing and provision of subsidised sites. These measures allow the local authority a range of options in addressing the housing needs of our citizens.

In recent years we have witnessed a sharp increase in the cost of private housing and this has limited the choices of our citizens in meeting their housing requirements. Local authorities will need to be innovative and flexible in meeting the challenge of ensuring that every citizen has access to good quality, affordable housing. Although these are complex issues I am confident that we will meet the challenge efficiently and imaginatively.

Introduction of County Managers

By the 1930s the need was perceived at government level to strengthen the administration of local government. This partly stemmed from a questioning of the need for local administrative bodies following independence, and tensions between central and local government where the latter were coming to be seen as wasting public money. A Department of Local Government memorandum of March 1934 stated that with the

> establishment of a Central Administration responsible to the people as a whole and with modern improvements in transport and communications, governmental intervention and supervision is now feasible in respect of all national activities. The retention of local government bodies is, therefore, gradually becoming an expensive anachronism.[4]

The memorandum went on to refer to the unsatisfactory conduct of local administration, financial maladministration and failure to fulfil duties and to comply with the law. While reform proposals were not pursued at the time, the need to reform the system remained and by 1940 it had been decided to appoint county managers to each county council to take responsibility for the administration of local government affairs.

The functions of the council were divided into listed functions requiring the approval of the elected members (reserved functions) and all other functions (executive functions) which were the legal responsibility of the county manager. This extended to the whole country a system introduced for city administration in the 1920s and which was modelled on management systems in use in the United States. The first county managers were appointed in 1942 and the system survives largely intact to the present day.

Debates at the time indicate that the imposition of an executive with independent powers was resented and resisted by many elected representatives at the time. They were understandably concerned that the county manager would effectively be the Department of Local Government's agent and would sideline or undermine their position. Dr T F O'Higgins TD claimed that 'We are … perhaps witnessing the passing of local government in this country in the popularly accepted sense'.[5] Another deputy, James Everett TD, went even further, claiming that 'the position … will be that the County Manager will be the "yes-man" of the Department and that the Irish people now can well complain of the Hitlerism that is about to start in the twenty-six counties'.[6]

In practice the county managers quickly settled in and, with a few exceptions, won the respect and trust of the elected members of the council. In 1954 the Minister for Local Government

> … announced his intention of visiting every county and county borough to obtain first-hand information on the relations between managers and elected members and to discover 'any defects thought to be inherent in the management system or that have developed in practice'. In July 1954 O'Donnell also agreed to meet the chairmen of urban district councils and town commissioners.
>
> These consultations revealed that there was much wider support for county management than many critics had suggested.[7]

**Thomas David Sinnott,
Co. Manager 1942-1953**

**Thomas Francis Broe,
Co. Manager 1954-1976**

**Michael Noel Dillon,
Co. Manager 1976-1993**

This support was largely due to the calibre of officials selected for these positions at first filling and subsequently. Wexford County Council has been fortunate in the individuals given this responsibility. The very first county manager was T D Sinnott who was county manager from 1942 until 1953. A teacher by profession T D Sinnott had served with the Irish Volunteers with great distinction during the War of Independence. He worked as secretary to the Wexford Board of Health and Public Assistance from 1922 to 1942.

On his retirement in 1953 Mr Sinnott was succeeded as county manager by Thomas Broe who had previously been Clare County Manager following a distinguished career in local government in Limerick, Kilkenny and Carlow.

In 1976 Mr Broe was replaced by M N Dillon who started his career as a clerical officer with Cork County Council in 1955 and just over twenty years later had risen to the top position in local government service. Mr Dillon remained in Wexford until 1993 when he left to take up duty as Cork County Manager.

When I replaced Noel Dillon as Wexford County Manager I became only the fourth person to hold that position. The fact that the executive arm of Wexford County Council has been led by only four individuals over a period of fifty years illustrates one of the strengths of our system, which is the continuity and durability of our traditions and structures. The primary motivation for the introduction of the management system to local government was to ensure efficient and accountable local administration. The level of open accountability in our system, and the probity of our financial and administrative affairs, is evidence that this objective has been achieved. However the manager's leadership role has expanded beyond these early goals. Collins concluded that

> ... if local government has made a wider contribution it is because the managers have offered leadership in policy innovation, formulation and direction. The contribution of elected politicians has been to legitimise that leadership and to facilitate the execution of policy by intervening on behalf of aggrieved citizens.[8]

Our management system has been examined from outside the state by Dr A H Marshall in work commissioned by the Maud committee on Management in Local Government in Britain. He sums up:

> The undeniable fact is that Ireland, having sought for an answer to the problem of reconciling ultimate democratic control with prompt discharge of duties, has found a solution which under Irish conditions is working well.[9]

However, the underlying strength of the management system lies in the ability it has demonstrated to create an essential partnership with the elected members. Although the legal position is one of rigid demarcation between the reserved powers of members and the executive powers of the manager, in practice the issue is rarely so clear-cut. Both arms of the system must, and do, work co-operatively to the benefit of the citizen.

Separating from Health

Until the 1970s local government, in addition to its other functions, had responsibility for the administration of the health services. The Health Act 1970 set up new health boards which took over these functions. This was tremendously significant at the time because the health services accounted for about one-third of all local government activity. The pressure to change the system did not arise from any deficiency in local government's stewardship and indeed the government moved very slowly before altering existing arrangements. Concerning this reluctance Hensey comments:

> The answer may be that there was a reluctance to take health administration away from the local government system because, whatever doubts there may have been about the effectiveness of the local authorities in the nineteen-forties, it was clear, once the county management system had settled down, that the county councils and other health authorities provided, within the confines of the counties, a good system of administration and one which should not be tampered with without very good reason.[10]

However by 1970 the case for changing the health structures was very strong. Health and local government had been divided into separate state departments as far back as 1947. By the 1960s hospital services were increasingly being centralised on a regional basis and local government, based as it was on the county, was increasingly seen as being an inappropriate vehicle to administer them.

Since their establishment the health boards have been very successful in developing and delivering high quality healthcare to the Irish people. Unless the local government system were to be altered in a fundamental way it is unlikely that local authorities could acquire the size and scale needed to administer effectively hospital services as is done in other countries. However, it might be argued that regional structures are not necessarily the best for all health services. Many community based services might be more attuned to local need if they were managed at a local level. There are also areas of overlap, such as the issue of food safety and public health nuisances, and these services might be managed by the local government system if the devolution of new functions to our system gains momentum. At the least the matter merits discussion and consideration.

Planning for Growth

The changes in the management structures introduced during the Second World War prepared the system for the difficulties of managing the development pressures that the post-war period was to bring. The pressure to build adequate infrastructure has been referred to above. After a period of recession in the 1950s the early 1960s saw an intense focus on economic development. Local government's main role in this process was through the development of a physical planning control system. The development pressures of the sixties highlighted the deficiencies in existing systems, which had been hidden by the economic stagnation and population decline, through emigration, of the 1950s. Only in Dublin was there a formal planning control scheme in place and many local authorities had no formal planning control at all.

To address this need the Local Government (Planning and Development) Act 1963 was passed and contains many of the features of planning control familiar to us today. However, it is interesting to note that one of the primary motivations for the introduction of the legislation was not only to strengthen planning control but to facilitate development, particularly in urban centres, and the legislation was designed to give local authorities wider powers to acquire land for development purposes. In introducing the Bill the minister stated that one of its main objects was

> To enable local authorities to facilitate industrial and commercial developments and to secure the redevelopment of those parts of built-up areas which have become outmoded, uneconomic or congested.[11]

The establishment of eighty-seven new planning authorities, each required to produce a development plan, exceeded the staff resources trained in planning then available in Ireland. However, extensive training and education of existing officers succeeded in meeting the need and the system was successfully introduced in 1964.

The planning process has expanded rapidly since its introduction, both in terms of numbers and complexity. In 1998 Wexford County Council received 2950 planning applications and this figure is expected to increase in 1999.

The introduction of development plans provided the framework for development by local authorities and private developers and allows developers to anticipate the type of development that is acceptable in the area. They also provide an opportunity for the local authority to examine strategically the needs of the county over a five year period. I believe that development plans have been an invaluable aid to the proper planning and development of our environment. However they have yet to reach their full potential as they remain heavily local authority oriented. The new mechanisms outlined in *Better Local Government – A Programme for Change* may provide an opportunity to broaden the scope of the development plan and permit it to play its full part in the local authorities' strategic planning process. In particular the development plan should encompass economic and social considerations in addition to physical planning.

The task of facilitating and encouraging development while at the same time protecting our environment is a complex one and is likely to become more so as time passes. However the responsibility for the proper planning and development of our county is one which we welcome and this task will remain one of our major functions in the new century.

Economic Development

One of the principal objectives of the Local Government (Planning and Development) Act 1963 was to facilitate local authorities in encouraging industrial and economic development.[12] The enhancement of the development role of the council was greatly welcomed and has remained a dominant concern of county

Urban renewal schemes, commenced in the 1980s, have made a valuable contribution to the regeneration of our towns.

managers since. The role was further clarified by the 1971 White Paper, *Local Government Reorganisation*, which stated that 'Local Authorities therefore must now regard themselves and be regarded as development corporations for their areas'.

In practice however it has been difficult for local government to live up to this role. Although the reasons for this are complex the fundamental difficulty has been that the local authority was assigned a role for which it was not equipped either in terms of financial resources or adequate powers. Roche states:

> The expression *development corporation* derives from British legislation on the creation of new towns, and signifies a state body with extensive powers of land acquisition and development: constructing roads, streets and open spaces; houses, flats, shops, offices, factories and all of the components of a town; providing services and (at least for a time) managing the properties so created. The project involves very heavy capital investment, supplied by the state. No Irish local authority is in a position to take on and accomplish an undertaking of this magnitude.[13]

As a consequence of the above, and the failure to integrate the resources of public and semi-state bodies with the local authorities' planning policies, the activities of local authorities in a planning context have been heavily weighted towards the physical planning control mechanisms rather than development oriented. The result has been a system more reactive than proactive and in many respects this has represented a missed opportunity for us.

However, notwithstanding the initial difficulties, local government's development activities have expanded significantly in recent years. The urban renewal schemes commenced in the late 1980s have provided a valuable opportunity to make a real contribution to the regeneration of our towns. I am aware that the schemes have considerable economic implications for the state due to the generous tax concessions included in the package. I am convinced however that the outstanding progress made in urban development would not have occurred without the impetus generated by the urban renewal schemes. In Wexford the major refurbishment of Wexford and Enniscorthy town centres is testimony to their success and it is notable that the regenerative process is extending outwards into undesignated areas, being driven by the economic development which has occurred. I am hopeful that similar progress will be made with the seaside resort scheme in Courtown and the urban renewal scheme in New Ross.

'Better Local Government – A Programme for Change'

In 1996 the government published its policy document on the strengthening of the local government system, *Better Local Government – A Programme for Change*. This followed on from thirty years of consideration of how local government ought to function in a modern state, beginning with the Devlin Report in the 1960s.

The policy document addressed the need for reform under the main headings of enhancing democracy, widening the role of local government, improving the quality of services to the customer, and the human resource, organisational and financial changes necessary to underpin these measures.

At national level it has been demonstrated that partnership between the different interests in society can bring enormous advantages over the more traditional adversarial approach. Much of our recent economic success as a nation can be directly attributed to the development of partnership structures between the government and the social partners. This does not diminish the legitimate leadership role of the government in our society. If we can duplicate this type of partnership at local level we can regenerate local government and develop structures and actions which will command support across our community.

Better Local Government stated the following:

> No single actor – public, private or voluntary body – has the knowledge or resources to tackle problems by unilateral action. Representative democracy can be strengthened by the involvement of local people in a meaningful way in devising new approaches to community needs. Such involvement and participation can represent a major resource available to councillors in carrying out their functions.[14]

Better Local Government led to the setting up of Strategic Policy Committees in each council. These committees will be responsible for drafting policy in all areas of the council's operations and for reporting to the council on policy implementation. Uniquely, however, community and sectoral groups will be directly represented on these committees where their nominees will sit alongside the elected members of the council and will be involved in drawing up policies from the earliest stages. The potential of these structures to ensure stronger and better policy formulation, and to generate widespread community support for these policies, is apparent. The committees will be serviced by directors of services who will ensure that they are given every necessary support to achieve their objectives.

In recent years a variety of agencies has been established to develop economic and social development in the community. These agencies include ADM Partnerships, County Enterprise Boards and LEADER Groups. These groups are well resourced from national and European sources and they have been very active and innovative in their respective areas.

However, to date, the local development agencies have operated apart from the local government system and this runs counter to current European thinking and experience among our European neighbours. It was also questioned whether these separate agencies, operating independently, were in the best interests of the consumer who, perhaps, found the system difficult to comprehend. The government examined these issues and *Better Local Government – A Programme for Change* signalled that local government and local development systems needed to be integrated. The resulting task force set up to advance these proposals found that there was considerable overlap between the agencies themselves. In its report it indicated that there were problems requiring attention.

> Nevertheless, it is now widely suggested, not least by the Partnership 2000 Pillars consulted, that there are overlaps between the functions carried out and the needs being addressed by the various local development organisations. Equally, it is felt that there are other areas where needs are not being fully addressed by any of the bodies.[15]

The report recommends that the existing county strategy groups be developed into county development boards by 1 January 2000. The boards will operate autonomously but under the local government umbrella and will be chaired by county council nominees. The primary purpose of each board will be to draw up and implement a strategy for economic, social and cultural development within the county. The membership of each board will consist of the chairpersons of the strategic policy committees, the county manager, the local development agencies, social partners, voluntary and community groups and relevant state agencies.

The process of developing these new mechanisms promises to be an exciting and challenging one and I look forward to working with all interested groups in establishing genuine and enduring partnerships which can work most effectively for the benefit of our community.

In recent years Wexford County Council, like all public authorities, has been working under the *Strategic Management Initiative* (SMI) to reform and renew the public service. The emphasis of the SMI is to improve the quality of the service to the public while also ensuring value for money in the services provided. The commitment to improving the quality of our services is most welcome. Perhaps more than any other arm of the state local government is sensitive to, and must respond positively to, the wishes of its customers.

Today's citizen demands, and has a right to expect, services of the highest quality from its public agencies. I believe that we have consistently striven to provide such services but there is always room for improvement. Wexford County Council is constantly seeking ways to improve its services, as demonstrated in recent years with the designation of our motor tax department under the ISO 9002 quality standard. We were the first local authority to achieve this award and it reflects the importance that Wexford County Council attaches to providing a high quality service to our customers.

We need to review all services to ensure that they reflect a customer-centred ethos and are provided as close to the customer as possible. Flexibility will be needed in all departments to ensure that this principle is central to our operations. The necessity of integrating the services of the county and urban authorities must also be addressed to ensure that the customer receives a seamless service at the point of delivery of the service. The Lacey Report stated that

> There is now an expectation and indeed an insistence on the part of the public on the best possible quality public service. That service must be convenient, efficient and comprehensive. It must not be affected by the complexities or idiosyncrasies derived from internal details of the local government system, such as the difference in functional responsibilities between different local authorities.[16]

It is clear therefore that the separation of service delivery between authorities based on boundary lines must be minimised wherever possible. All local authorities are mandated by *Better Local Government* to place quality customer services at the centre of their strategic planning and the Wexford local authorities will continue to pursue this objective in our county.

Partnership with our Community

The central strength of local government is its place in the local community. The local council, democratically elected, can lead and support the community in projects important to them. The elected members of the council, and the staff living and working in the community, are particularly sensitive and responsive to these issues.

Extensive partnership already takes place across a wide variety of areas. Wexford County Council routinely interacts with business, farming, tourism, environmental and community groups in connection with its activities and services. The members of the council have consistently supported partnership with community based groups, lending assistance to ensure success in joint initiatives. Frequently we are not the primary force behind these projects but are content to assist where needed. In the last decade the council has allocated over £2 million in direct aid to community initiatives. In addition the council has been involved in the direct provision of projects such as the Irish National Heritage Park which was developed by Wexford County Council in the late 1980s to provide an attraction to service our tourism industry. We also give direct assistance, both financial and staffing, to community initiatives. Each year Wexford County

The Irish National Heritage Park at Ferrycarrig is an outdoor museum containing reproductions and reconstructions of sites and buildings depicting settlement in Ireland from 7000 BC to the twelfth century AD. Picture shows stone circle with round tower and Norman fortification in background.

The Viking boatyard at the Irish National Heritage Park, Ferrycarrig.

Council allocates approximately £250,000 in direct aid to worthy community projects.

Our involvement during 1998 with the Comóradh '98 commemorations is an excellent example of the potential of the local government system to support community activity and to exercise a multiplier effect where the outcome far exceeds the original input by the council.

As far back as 1988 the local authorities in Wexford organised a committee, Comóradh '98, to ensure an appropriate commemoration of the 1798 rebellion. The rebellion was a hugely traumatic affair in the county with over 30,000 people killed in only four weeks. Its true purpose and objectives had also been obscured by partisan propaganda during the nineteenth century.

Local authorities began contributing annually to a fund to finance the building of a 1798 centre in Enniscorthy which would accurately portray the context, actions and outcomes of the rebellion. The community was invited to participate in the work of the committee and it soon became an active and energetic vehicle which harnessed widespread community support.

When 1998 arrived Comóradh '98 was ready with an astounding array of activities to research and explore the context of the rebellion and to place it in perspective for a modern society. These events included:

- the building of the national 1798 visitor centre in Enniscorthy. Costing £2.5 million the centre was opened on 5 June 1998 and received over 60,000 visitors by the end of the year

The National 1798 Visitor Centre at Enniscorthy, officially opened on 5 June 1998 by An Taoiseach, Bertie Ahern.

- over 100 lectures on the Rebellion, held mostly in Wexford but also as far away as Australia, Canada, USA and the UK
- a calendar of events throughout the county, organised by local communities under the umbrella of Comóradh '98. Over sixty plaques were erected and three major monuments unveiled
- seventy-three books were published and three major television programmes were organised
- the reconvening of the Wexford Senate brought together almost 500 senators from Wexford and around the world whose generous financial support contributed to the National 1798 Centre project
- parishes throughout the county organised troops of pikemen who trained and drilled in the early part of the year to be ready for the commemorations. Marching in uniform, they attended community events which reached their peak on 21 June when over 3000 pikemen marched behind their parish banners over a six mile route to Vinegar Hill to mark the anniversary of the battle there in 1798.

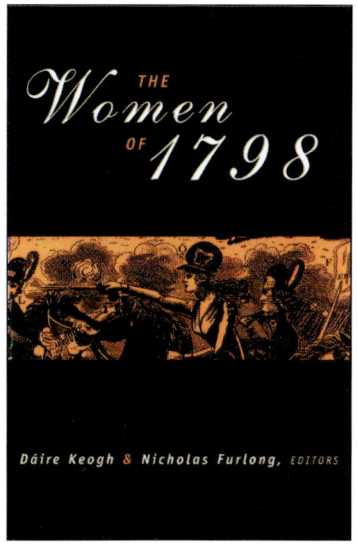

Although 1998 is over, the rise in community spirit is still apparent throughout the county. There is a new confidence in Wexford people which is based on a feeling of accomplishment and community pride in a job well done. These achievements would not have been possible without the involvement of the whole community in the project. Equally however they would not have been possible without the foresight and leadership shown by local authorities in the county in seeing the need and developing the structures and resources required.

I am extremely confident that the development of this kind of partnership with the community will allow local government to generate the support and commitment it will need in meeting the challenges ahead.

Looking to the Future

Our record over the one hundred years since the council was established is one of progress and achievement. We have been successful in meeting the demands placed on us. Most of the infrastructure essential to modern life, piped water, sewers and road networks were built by local authorities during this period. Our public housing programmes are largely responsible for eradicating the slum conditions common earlier this century. Our successes have been due to the dedication of the elected members of the council through the years and to the efforts of the staff who have served the council with loyalty and commitment. However the fact that we have succeeded in meeting the needs of the past does not guarantee that we will be successful in the next millennium.

The rapidly growing economy is placing heavy demands on our existing infrastructure and these demands will grow significantly over the next ten years. A deficit in this area is already being identified as a strategic weakness likely to inhibit the type of economic growth rates we have experienced in the 1990s. Local government will need to be able to respond to these demands in a timely and efficient manner if we are to maintain our proud tradition in this area.

1798 publications.

Section of new bridge being lifted into place, Wexford 1997.

However, I believe that if we are to continue to play a central role in our communities we must look beyond our traditional services. Our future role needs to be more than infrastructure providers or local agencies for central services. Valuable as these roles are they do not represent the full potential of the local government system and I believe that we have far more than that to offer our citizens.

Our central role in the next century will be as providers of services which are needed and valuable to our citizens. With the exception of Dáil Éireann the local authority is the only arm of the state directly elected by the people. This confers a legitimate leadership role on local government and gives us a mandate for direct intervention in the community for the benefit of our citizens. However to be truly effective we need to be able to harness the goodwill and support of the community.

The new structures introduced by *Better Local Government* will provide a vehicle to ensure that we can adapt ourselves to the realities of a society in the twenty-first century. There are developments in the community that can help us in this regard. There is a growing trend of participation by individuals in groups active on particular issues, e.g. the environment, or in their local areas in a voluntary capacity. These individuals may not be interested in participating directly in the political process but they bring a wealth of ability and experience into the service of their community through their voluntary efforts. If this dynamism can be allied with the formal democratic leadership of the local government system the result will be a powerful force for mobilising the wider community for the betterment of our county. The strategic policy committees will facilitate this.

I am optimistic about the future of local government as we reach the end of our first century. Local authorities are working hard to improve the quality and effectiveness of our services and the value for money we offer our citizens. We are responding to their desire for more open and accountable structures and new provisions such as the Freedom of Information Act 1997 and better dissemination of information by councils through publications such as this one will assist this process. There is a desire in the community to be more closely involved in the work of the council, as evidenced by the huge enthusiasm to participate on the strategic policy committees. This will facilitate deepening of our partnership with the community and will benefit the local government system into the future.

We have come a long way since 1898 – as a nation, as a state and as a community. For perhaps the first time in our history we are facing the future with expectation and optimism, confident that we can meet the challenges ahead. Local government has played its full part in this transformation. In our early years local authorities represented the people when other means of national expression were denied. Later on we built the infrastructure which would eventually transform our community and social conditions. Today we provide a broad range of services to all of our citizens and interact frequently with state and other agencies on their behalf. At all times we have tried to represent the people, to whom we are directly responsible through the democratic process, to the best of our ability.

We now face times of change as we head into our second century. However I am confident that we will meet new challenges as we have met those of the past. We have a proud tradition and legacy to build on. I hope that when the history of our second century comes to be written the historians can say that our achievements were the equal of those who came before us.

**Seamus Dooley,
Co. Manager**

Notes

1. Local Government (Ireland) Act 1898, Section 22(1)
2. Quoted in Neil Collins, *Local Government Managers at Work*, IPA 1987 p 9
3. James Meenan, *The Irish Economy since 1922*, p 15
4. Quoted in *City and County Management 1929-1990*, IPA pp 14-15
5. Quoted in *The Buffer State – The Historical Roots of the Department of the Environment*, IPA 1997 p 304
6. Quoted in *City and County Management 1929-1990*, IPA 1991 pp 16-17
7. *The Buffer State – The Historical Roots of the Department of the Environment*, IPA 1997 p 316-17
8. Neil Collins, *Local Government Managers at Work*, IPA 1987 p 195
9. (A H Marshall) Committee on the Management of Local Government, 'Management of Local Government', vol. 4, *Local Government Administration Abroad*, London: Her Majesty's Stationery Office, 1967 p 24
10. Brendan Hensey, *The Health Services of Ireland*, IPA p 56
11. *Dáil Debates* vol. 197, 22 November 1962: 1771
12. See Local Government (Planning and Development) Act 1963 – explanatory memorandum p 1
13. Desmond Roche, *Local Government in Ireland*, p 135
14. *Better Local Government – A Programme for Change*, Department of the Environment p 20
15. Report of the Task Force on Integration of Local Government and Local Development Systems, August 1998 p 12
16. *Towards Cohesive Local Government – Town and County*, Reorganisation Commission, April 1996, Government Publications Office, 13.1 p 102

Views from the Council Chamber

Hugh Byrne TD, Fianna Fáil

I WAS FIRST ELECTED to Wexford County Council in 1974 and at each subsequent election up to and including my resignation in July 1997. I was proud to head the poll on all four occasions and to follow in the footsteps of my grandfather, James Byrne, as a member of the council. I believe that my chairmanship of the council in 1991 was a positive one. It allowed me to chair the New Ross Harbour Board (now the New Ross Port Company) at a time of great change and development. Further infrastructural development and investment was carried out on other harbours within the county. Particular mention must be made of Kilmore Quay and the overall investment of £3.5 million.

The work of local authorities can be taken for granted at times but I believe that any rational analysis of council policy, particularly in the New Ross district, will be favourable. Whether it be in the area of housing or roads or traveller accommodation, I believe that the policies pursued by myself and my fellow councillors will stand up to scrutiny. I was particularly keen to see the council become more involved in the community sector. This has seen the local authorities develop initiatives in relation to Duncannon Fort, Fethard Castle and Hook Head heritage. The link into the community sector is vital to the relevancy of the county council.

Over the years I was delighted to be involved with the provision of the Passage/Ballyhack car ferry and the National Heritage Park. I would like to

Council meeting in council chamber, County Hall, Wexford.

remember in particular Tommy Howlin, Jim Bowe and Pat McDonald for their service to the county. It is also fitting to mention past county managers, T F Broe and Noel Dillon. All of these people in conjunction with members both past and present have given great service to the county. Long may it continue.

Ivan Yates TD, Fine Gael

Wexford County Council has been the umbrella body and engine for the development of the county. Not only are there many of its physical, historical achievements of infrastructure around the county but the council has also spawned many successful developmental initiatives. The high quality of roads, bridges, sanitary-service schemes, water schemes and public housing has left an indelible mark on the county. Furthermore, the initiatives in the area of tourism, small business development, the arts, the library services and the fire services have often been beyond the level of statutory requirement.

One has only to think of the ownership and responsibility the council took in the development of the National Heritage Park at Ferrycarrig and the 1798 National Interpretative Centre in Enniscorthy to see permanent, indelible monuments to its commitment to enhancing the county. Moreover, there has always been a positive attitude by both members and officials of Wexford County Council to acting in partnership with private enterprise to stimulate development. This is evidenced in industrial parks, harbour-related investments and urban renewal schemes. The ethos of public service by the officials of the council has been outstanding. This has blended with the foresight and courage of council members who individually and collectively have shown commitment over successive decades in the advancement of the county. This has resulted in Wexford being one of the most attractive places in Ireland to live, or to visit as a holiday destination. The aim of future generations must be to maintain the high standards set heretofore by both members and officials.

Seán Doyle, Non-Party, Enniscorthy Electoral Area

It is my considered opinion that members of the public of County Wexford are not shaking with anticipatory delight at the thought of celebrating the centenary of local government in Ireland. Most of us in local government are aware of the general lack of interest in our activities. This apathetic attitude exists in spite of the fact that the activities and decisions of Wexford County Council and other local authorities within the county, impinge on all our lives.

Decisions of central government have resulted in very few people in the county contributing directly to the coffers of the county council. Commercial premises pay rates and water charges. The rest of us pay for certain services such as refuse collection and fees for planning permission. If the government is serious about local government, it must devolve power from the centre to local control. If that happens, it will be incumbent upon the local public representative to give responsible leadership and to indicate that he or she is capable of handling extra power and responsibility for the common good. I have a belief that neither central government nor the civil service trust us. Trust us and do something constructive to commemorate the birth of local government in Ireland.

Paddy Kavanagh, Fine Gael, Enniscorthy Electoral Area

As a public body, Wexford County Council has served the people of County Wexford well over the last one hundred years. Through the various committees covering all aspects of social and economic life, the public representatives and council officials have guided the county through good times and bad. As a newly selected councillor (October 1998), I feel the authority has lost a lot of its powers in recent years. If central government was to put local government and the county councillor centre stage at local level, I feel confident that we as a body have the ability, the vision and the local knowledge to guide this Model County of ours into the next century.

Finally, on such an historic occasion as this, let us not forget all the past members of this body, staff and councillors alike, people from all walks of life and all political persuasions, who have contributed to make this council work so well over the last one hundred years. *Go raibh míle maith agaibh.*

**Leo Carthy, Non-Party, Wexford Electoral Area,
Chairman 1998-1999**

Deirdre Bolger, Fine Gael, Gorey Electoral Area

As Wexford County Council marks its centenary, we can reflect with pride on the sound principles which have been responsible for the successful development of this Model County. Environmental awareness, consumer needs, a social conscience and commercial orientation have been the foundations of every decision. Co-operation between elected members and administration has undoubtedly achieved much for the betterment of Wexford. Forward planning, innovative and unimpeded vision placed the county in a strategic position to take advantage of the changing times and economic climate. My twenty-one years of service as a member of Wexford County Council have been most fulfilling. I have no doubt that the challenges of the next millennium will be equally rewarding for those who serve to maximise the opportunities of the new and exciting technological age.

**John Bolger, Fine Gael,
Enniscorthy Electoral Area**

**John A Browne TD, Fianna Fáil,
Enniscorthy Electoral Area**

**Seán Doyle, Non-Party,
Enniscorthy Electoral Area**

**Patrick Kavanagh, Fine Gael,
Enniscorthy Electoral Area**

**Michelle Sinnott, Fianna Fáil,
Enniscorthy Electoral Area**

Rory Murphy, Fianna Fáil, Gorey Electoral Area

In the past one hundred years, many men and women have offered themselves for election as members of Wexford County Council. About half of those who contended were elected to serve and to represent their district on the premier ruling body in the county. Each saw his or her role from a different perspective. Some saw it to be the making of the best possible laws and bye-laws for the better order of the functions entrusted to them. Others saw their role as one of getting the most benefit for the districts they represented.

In the century since its foundation, the role and function of the council has changed. Its source of revenue altered dramatically when rates were removed from domestic dwellings and later from agricultural land. Other means of funding statutory activities had to be found. This was done successfully though not always

**Lorcan Allen, Fianna Fáil,
Gorey Electoral Area**

**Deirdre Bolger, Fine Gael,
Gorey Electoral Area**

**Michael J D'Arcy TD, Fine Gael,
Gorey Electoral Area**

**James Gahan, Fine Gael,
Gorey Electoral Area**

**Rory Murphy, Fianna Fáil,
Gorey Electoral Area**

without a hard fight. The county finances are now, largely, in balance.

Not everybody has a good feeling about the council and its activities. This is true of all organisations from time to time and we must be content to live with it. That 'there are no rewards and no penalties, there are only consequences' is basically true and many a councillor who had served well was rejected at a subsequent election.

Local franchise is a precious thing to our democracy. For many hundreds of years our fate lay in the hands of those who had little to commend them but their own self-interest. The first vestige of local democracy came in the form of the poor law guardians whose function lay in the management of the workhouses and in local health matters. It was for election to these bodies that electoral divisions were established. In 1898, command of the affairs of the county was transferred from the grand juries (drawn from the landowners and others of the propertied classes) to a

**John T Browne, Fine Gael,
New Ross Electoral Area**

**James Curtis, Fianna Fáil,
New Ross Electoral Area**

**Laurence O'Brien, Fine Gael,
New Ross Electoral Area**

**James Walsh, Senator, Fianna Fáil,
New Ross Electoral Area**

**Seamus Whelan, Fianna Fáil,
New Ross Electoral Area**

council elected by open franchise.

Success is best measured by what is achieved, not by length of service. With an excellent team of officials and an above average set of councillors, Wexford is well poised to remain at the forefront of local administration in its second century.

John T Browne, Fine Gael, New Ross Electoral Area

Having been a member of Wexford County Council for almost twenty years, I am very aware of the many valuable and worthwhile projects that have been initiated in that time. Substantial progress has been made in house building, road construction, water schemes, sewage works and other ancillary schemes.

While there have been difficulties, both financially and politically, in achieving all the aims the council sets out in its annual programme, it must be conceded that

**Gus Byrne, Fianna Fáil,
Wexford Electoral Area**

**Thomas Carr, Labour,
Wexford Electoral Area**

**Leo Carthy, Non-Party,
Wexford Electoral Area**

**Pat Codd, Fine Gael,
Wexford Electoral Area**

**John O'Flaherty, Fianna Fáil,
Wexford Electoral Area**

**Padge Reck, Non-Party,
Wexford Electoral Area**

the unanimous support of the members, together with the commitment of management and officials, has brought about some dramatic and worthwhile benefits for the whole community in County Wexford.

It is to be hoped that, as we approach the millennium, and having celebrated the centenary of the council, new ideas and ventures will be realised, and that with a strong and vibrant county council, Wexford will remain the Model County.

Gus Byrne, Fianna Fáil, Wexford Electoral Area

Over thirty years ago my interest in local government was stimulated by men such as Dr James Ryan, Jimmy Kennedy and Seán Browne, all of whom have now passed on. Their commitment was tremendous and for me it was inspirational. In March 1974 I was co-opted to Wexford Corporation and in 1979 I was elected to both Wexford Corporation and County Council. I am very thankful to all those people who put me there.

Since then local government has changed and probably will never cease to change. To have been part of that movement of expansion and part of what has been achieved gives one the will and motivation to fashion the Wexford that we all want to see. The future of the county is, after all, everyone's concern. As we move towards a new century and a new millennium, we are putting a worthwhile infrastructure in place in the county. The major areas of progress include: urban renewal, Rosslare Harbour, Kilmore Harbour, the main drainage and sewage schemes, Fardystown water-supply scheme, the reconstruction of Wexford bridge, and various town by-pass schemes. Many projects are ongoing and the best of Rosslare Harbour is still to come. While there is a lot of work still to be done, Wexford is highly placed on any list of top counties. The flavour of '98 and its outstanding year's programme of events raised our standing even higher and will be remembered for many years to come.

John O'Flaherty, Fianna Fáil, Wexford Electoral Area

Over the last one hundred years, Wexford County, under the direction and control of Wexford County Council, has expanded and developed out of all recognition in every facet of its services. The councillors, together with an expert technical and administrative staff, are providing a professional service of the highest quality, particularly in the areas of house building, road construction and maintenance, harbour development, sewage services, water supply and conservation.

Arts and cultural development are catered for in a special way. We operate an excellent library service which is much appreciated and used in both urban and rural areas. The service is to get a new Wexford branch and headquarters in the near future.

Value for money in all that we do is the priority of the councillors. May the progress and development in the coming years reflect the achievements of the past.

Padge Reck, Non-Party, Wexford Electoral Area

The modern concept of Irish local government at county level dates back to 1898 when the British government of the day decided to give locally elected people the power to raise revenue within their own counties and to spend that money improving the infrastructure of the county. From a councillor's perspective, there have been three major changes within the last one hundred years, each in its own way having a profound effect on the system and its operation. The power of the elected members to raise funds and the authority to spend that revenue remained intact until the introduction of the county managerial system to the county in 1942. Under the new system a division of powers was instituted: the county manager was given executive powers while the members were charged with responsibility for what were called reserved functions.

Among the reserved functions entrusted to councillors were the power to strike the rate and the power to adopt the county development plan. The power to strike the rate frequently produced friction within the council chamber. The councillors were required by law to raise the necessary funding to run the affairs of the county. However, this could not be done without inflicting a certain degree of pain on the rate payer. There were twenty-one councillors, some urban, some rural, some farmers, some business people, each in turn protecting the interests of his or her electorate while mindful of the consequences of not striking the rate. This was a serious element of local government because the minister reserved the right to abolish a council if it failed to strike a rate.

The second significant change to the local government system was the abolition of rates on domestic dwellings. In the general election campaign of 1977 the incoming government committed itself to the abolition of domestic rates and their replacement with a direct subvention from the state. It was a decision which impacted severely on all local authorities. Those who warned against it were completely ignored until 1983 when the state realised it could not continue to finance local authorities. However, the county council still managed to keep water flowing through taps, refuse continued to be collected and roads were maintained.

The third and latest change to the system came in late 1998 with the introduction of special policy committees. For the first time in over one hundred years, the elected members will be working in council committees with non-elected community representatives to focus on recommendations in policy formulation and to encourage community support for policy implementation. Some councillors may see these special policy committees as mere talking shops because they have no powers other than to recommend change. Others, however, see them as a real opportunity to illustrate to the outside bodies the financial constraints facing the local authority. They may also expect those nominees to appreciate how difficult it is to balance the books in the modern system of local government. It will also give an opportunity to those appointed from outside the system to recognise the value of a county manager and a team of officials, working together with twenty-one public representatives, who have collectively given us an infrastructure of which we can be proud.

COUNTY MANAGERS' CONFERENCE - JANUARY, 1943

Front row, L to R: J P. Flynn (Tipperary NR and SR); D C Murphy (Louth); W F Quinlan (Kerry);

E A Joyce (Carlow/Kildare); P J Bartley (Laois/Offaly); P J. Meghen (Limerick)

Second row, L to R: M J Egan (Mayo); C I Flynn (Galway); J G Browne (Roscommon): P T Healy (Wicklow)

Third row, L to R: P McGeough (Monaghan); M A Veale (Cavan); S D MacLochlainn (Donegal);

T Hayes (Longford/Westmeath); S J Moynihan (Kilkenny/Waterford)

Back row, L to R: J F Wrenne (Cork); D O'Keeffe (Clare); J Hurley (Meath); T D Sinnott (Wexford)

County Managers

The county management system has its origins in the reforming measures introduced to local government in the early and uncertain years of independent Ireland. At that time many councils stood accused of discharging their public business in a partisan, corrupt and inefficient manner. In 1925, the Free State government, in an attempt to curb the activities of these councils and to repair the damaged reputation of local government, introduced a new Local Government Act. The Act gave extensive powers to the Minister for Local Government to enquire into the conduct of a council and to dissolve it if such an enquiry showed that this action was necessary in the public interest. Out of this provision came what Basil Chubb in *A source book of Irish government* describes as 'perhaps Ireland's major invention in the field of government'.

The 1925 Act allowed that where a council was dissolved the minister could appoint commissioners to exercise its duties for a period not exceeding three years. It was hoped that at the end of that period a new and more responsible council would be elected. This measure was intended to punish errant councils but it turned out to be extremely popular with the electorate. In some areas where councils were dissolved, voters simply refused to choose another council, thereby forcing central government to reappoint its commissioners.

Although the removal of administrative powers from local politicians was often condemned as profoundly undemocratic, the idea of an independently appointed, professional local administrator grew in popularity. In 1929 the city of Cork blazed a trail with the appointment of a city manager modelled to some extent on the existing commissioners but intended to work with the city council and not to replace it. Other cities soon followed Cork's example; Dublin (1930), Limerick (1934) and Waterford (1939). In 1940 the County Management Act extended the management system to the counties. Under the terms of the Act, all councils were obliged to have or to share a manager. The managers were to be appointed by the Local Appointments Commission and were to be permanent, full-time and salaried administrators. Although the financial and legal responsibilities of the elected members were maintained in a series of reserved functions, the Management Act brought about a significant shift in power from politicians to officials. Because he enjoyed the advantage of continuity, the manager – particularly if he had the rudiments of diplomacy – was in a position to influence very powerfully the course of local government within his county.

Wexford's first county manager was appointed in August 1942, the same month in which that year's local elections were held. There was a very small turnout at these elections, probably because they took place during harvesting. However, the local press suggested that the apathy among voters had another cause, the introduction of the management system. The *Free Press* of 29 August 1942 commented:

> The smallness of the voting everywhere reflects the lack of interest of the average rural elector. This lethargy may have been partly caused by the known fact that the county councils about to be elected would be stripped of so much of their responsibility for carrying on local public affairs.

The editorial went on to criticise the measure by which it claimed 'our own government is divesting our popularly elected councils of their authority and activities and transferring them to paid county managers. The old theory that good government is no substitute for self-government seems to have gone out of fashion'. Nevertheless, the press was prepared to refrain from further comment until this 'very great change in local administration [could] be judged on the way it works out'. In this atmosphere it is not surprising that the Local Appointments Commission should choose as Wexford's first county manager a man who not only had a proven track record in local government administration but was also a popular and well-regarded native of the county, Thomas David Sinnott.

Thomas David ('T D') Sinnott

Born in January 1893 at Ballyelland, Davidstown, T D Sinnott was the eldest son of John and Annie Sinnott. His father was prominent in the Land League and served for many years on the Enniscorthy Board of Guardians and on Enniscorthy Rural District Council. T D Sinnott was educated at Davidstown National School and later at Enniscorthy Christian Brothers' school. In 1913, following his registration as a secondary school teacher, he taught science at a school in Dundalk. About this time he became associated with the Irish Volunteers. After a year or two he returned to Enniscorthy where he took a prominent part in the Gaelic League and Sinn Fein. In 1916, having been one of the leaders of the Easter Rising in Enniscorthy, he was arrested and transported to England. He spent periods of detention in both Stafford Jail and Frongoch until his release under a general amnesty at Christmas 1916.

On his return to Enniscorthy, T D Sinnott opened a stationery and tobacco business in Rafter Street. In August 1918 he was arrested again and spent six months in Cork Jail. In 1920 he was elected to Enniscorthy Urban Council with a poll of two quotas and in June of that year he became chairman of the Enniscorthy Board of Guardians. However, later that year he was arrested again and after periods of detention in Waterford, Kilworth and Cork, he was interned in Ballykinlar camp, Belfast. In 1922, after the Free State was established, he was appointed secretary to the County Board of Health (later known as the Board of Health and Public Assistance), the successor to the boards of guardians and, after their abolition in 1925, to the rural district councils. It was in this position that he was to show his outstanding administrative skills in a number of major undertakings over the next twenty years.

Picture taken at County Hall, Wexford after the last meeting of the Wexford Board of Health and Public Assistance in August 1942.
Back row, L to R: P Dunbar, G Flood, J J Shortell, L O'Mahoney, R J Shortell, Thomas Redmond, T D Sinnott (Secretary), Patrick Colfer, P Ronan, J Lawlor, B Corish, P V Carson.
Seated, L to R: J Crosbie, Nellie Hore, Thomas McCarthy, Ald. Richard Corish TD, Nell O'Ryan, Denis Allen TD, Dr D McDonald, Asst County Medical Officer, Colonel R P Wemyss Quin.

Under T D Sinnott's administration the institutions formerly maintained by the boards of guardians were reorganised. This involved the closing of the old union workhouses and the setting up of the County Hospital in Wexford and St John's Hospital in Enniscorthy. Two new district hospitals were erected at New Ross and Gorey and a county fever hospital was established at New Ross. Brownswood house near Enniscorthy was purchased, reconstructed and equipped as an eighty-bed sanatorium. Considerable extensions and improvements were also carried out at St Senan's psychiatric hospital, Enniscorthy. In 1932, the Board of Health and Public Assistance began a major drive to provide housing in rural areas, a scheme that T D Sinnott was to continue in his years as county manager. From 1922 until his retirement in 1953, no less than 1,742 cottages were erected in rural County Wexford.

The District Hospital, Gorey, built by the Board of Health and Public Assistance.

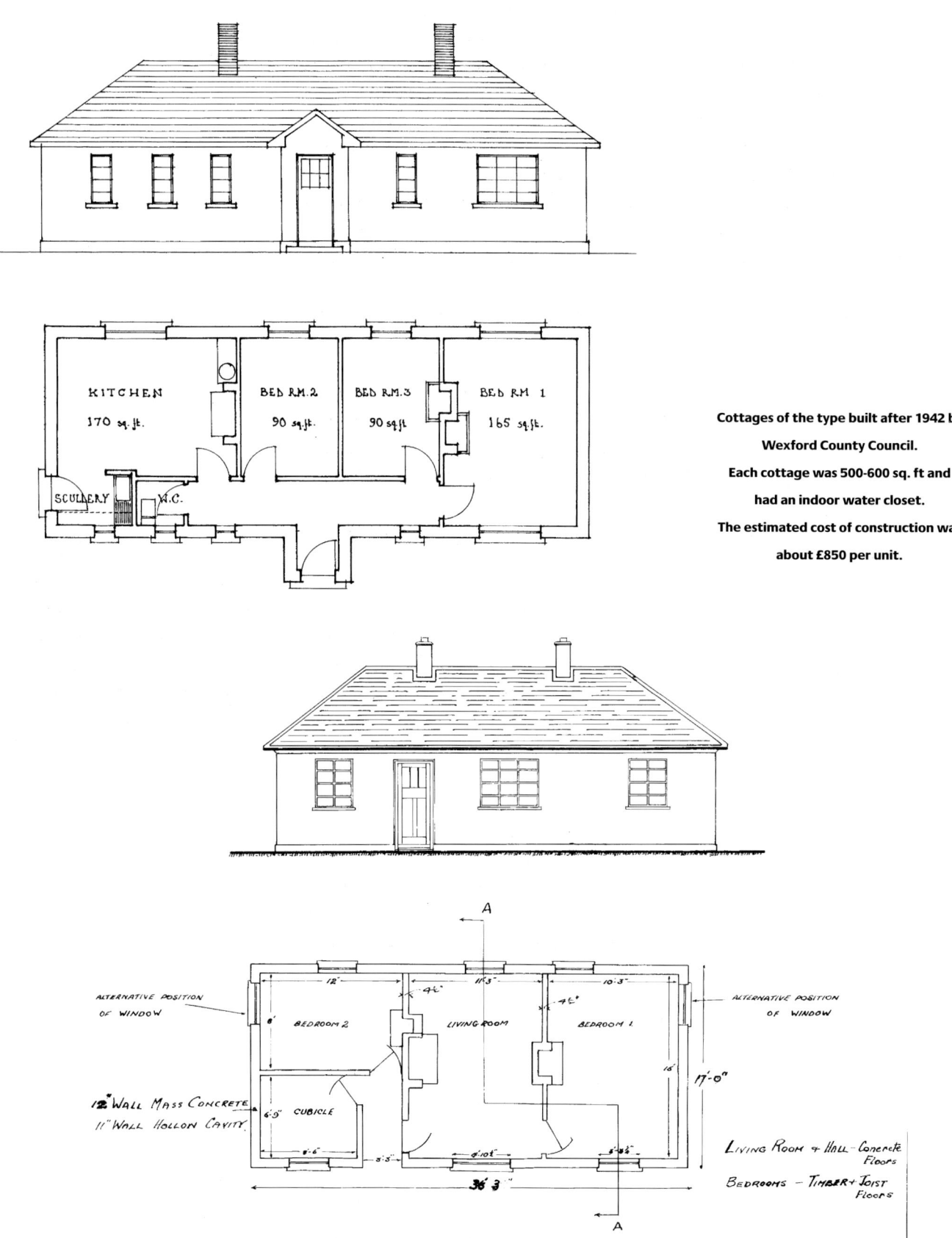

Cottages of the type built after 1942 by Wexford County Council. Each cottage was 500-600 sq. ft and had an indoor water closet. The estimated cost of construction was about £850 per unit.

In 1940 T D Sinnott was appointed county commissioner for the Emergency period and was also made first leader of the Local Defence Force on its establishment in June of that year. By the time he was appointed county manager in August 1942 he was already well known as a lecturer in local government procedures and administration. As county manager he continued the many housing and water-supply schemes begun during his period as secretary to the Board of Health and Public Assistance. He also initiated an imaginative project to plant apple trees along the roadsides of the county. In 1945 he was appointed by the government as its negotiator with the Lakin family for the handing over of Johnstown Castle to the state. Three years before his retirement he spearheaded an ambitious seven-year programme for the reconstruction of the county's rural roads.

T D Sinnott's interests were not confined to his work as a public official and there was scarcely a movement or organisation in the county with which he was not associated. In sporting life he was a founder member and president of the Wexford and District Coursing Club. He was also a leading figure in the establishment of Wexford Sports Ltd, the owners of the racecourse at Bettyville, Wexford. His work for the promotion of the Irish language and culture was well known. In 1920 he helped to establish an Irish-speaking camp for children in Ballyconnigar, Blackwater, which was a forerunner of *Coláiste Carman*, Gorey. His first order as county manager was to direct the county secretary to have a notice displayed in each office in County Hall inviting public and staff to conduct their business through Irish. He was also vice-president of the local branch of *Conradh na Gaeilge* and one of the chief organisers of *Feis Carman*.

The legacy of T D Sinnott's imaginative scheme of planting fruit trees along road margins was still to be seen in May 1970 when this group of cherry and apple trees on the Wexford-Rosslare road was photographed.

He had a deep interest in local history and was associated with both the *Uí Cinnsealaigh* Society and the Old Wexford Society. Widely regarded as an expert on the 1798 rebellion, he could trace family connections to Fr Michael Murphy of Ballycanew who was killed at the battle of Arklow and to the rebel Thomas Sinnott of Kilbride. He was also related to Fr Patrick Kavanagh the author of *A Popular History of the Insurrection of 1798*. In 1938 and 1948 he was heavily involved in organising the commemorative events to mark the anniversaries of the 1798 rebellion.

T D Sinnott was a prolific writer of prose and poetry in both English and Irish and contributed frequently to periodicals under the pen-name 'A K Killiane'. Many of his poems, such as *Sweet Slaneyside* and *To Mary and to Wexford true*, achieved considerable popularity. However, his best known work is entitled *Ninety-eight – a dramatic symposium* which was first performed at the Theatre Royal, Wexford in December 1937. Among his other publications is an article entitled 'Anglo-Irish poets and poetry in Wexford' which was first read as a paper to the Library Conference in Wexford in 1938.

When ill health forced his premature retirement in October 1953, representatives from many organisations and all political parties in the county paid warm tribute to T D Sinnott's service to his native county. However, even in retirement he was indefatigable. In 1959 he became chairman of the County Wexford Committee of the Irish Red Cross Society and organised its water safety section, first in Wexford town and later in Curracloe and other centres around the county's coast.

T D Sinnott, educator, poet, linguist, orator, historian and public administrator, died on 1 June 1965 and was buried with military honours in St Ibar's cemetery, Crosstown, Wexford. In June 1987 the council's public library headquarters at Abbey Street, Wexford was named *Teach Shionóid* in his memory. The Sinnott family's long tradition of involvement in the public life of the county was continued by T D Sinnott's nephew, Michael Sinnott of Crossabeg, who served as elected member of the council from 1974 until his death in March 1995. In June 1995, Michael Sinnott's daughter, Michelle was co-opted to her father's seat on the council.

Thomas Francis Broe

When T F Broe was appointed county manager for Wexford in June 1954 he brought to the position almost twenty years of experience in local government administration. Born in Kildare in September 1910, he was educated at Naas CBS and at University College Dublin from which he graduated with a degree in commerce. He first entered the public service in 1936 as an accountant with Kildare Board of Health. Subsequently, he worked as accountant with Carlow County Council (1940-42) and with Limerick County Council (1943-44). In September 1944 he took up duty as county secretary with Kilkenny County Council. In June 1946 he returned to Limerick County Council as county secretary. He remained in Limerick until May 1952 when he was appointed county manager in Clare, a position he held until his appointment as Wexford's second county manager.

During his term as Wexford's county manager, T F Broe took a special interest in the provision of health services. He spearheaded a major reconstruction and refurbishment of St Senan's hospital, Enniscorthy, an extension to the county hospital and the construction of the county clinic at Grogan's Road, Wexford. He expanded T D Sinnott's programme of road development and initiated several bridge-building projects including Wexford Bridge (1959) and O'Hanrahan Bridge, New Ross (1967). He was instrumental in modernising the water-supply system in the county, introducing tap water to many homes where previously a hand pump was the only means of supply.

Postcard of Wexford's 'new' bridge, 1960.

Opening of Wexford bridge, 1959.

Development in planning regulations, an increase in house construction, the provision of swimming pools in Wexford and New Ross and the setting up of the county development team all owed much to T F Broe's progressive and foresighted policies. On his initiative Wexford County Council acquired a computer and became the first county council to do so. He saw clearly the importance of planning and development, not only for County Wexford but for the south-east region, and he became one of the founder-members of the South East Regional Development Organisation.

Kennedy Memorial Swimming Pool, New Ross.

T F Broe was highly regarded in local government circles throughout Ireland as an able and experienced administrator. His consummate skill as a negotiator and diplomat, threading his way through often difficult council meetings, was underpinned by his courteous, unassuming and patient manner. In tributes paid to him on his retirement in May 1976 he was repeatedly referred to by both elected members and staff as 'a perfect gentleman'. In May 1985 T F Broe died in Limerick where he was serving on an interview panel for the Mid-Western Health Board. He is buried in St Ibar's cemetery, Crosstown, Wexford.

First accounting machine acquired by the county council, a Hollerith.

Noel Dillon

When Michael Noel Dillon took up duty as Wexford County Manager on 1 June 1976, he was only the third person to hold the office since its establishment in 1942. Both his predecessors, T D Sinnott and T F Broe, had distinguished careers with many fine achievements. It quickly became obvious, however, that Noel Dillon had his own style and that the delivery of traditional services was to be open to embellishment with new ideas and changes of emphasis.

Born in Cork city in 1936, Noel Dillon entered the local government service in 1955 with Cork County Council and later moved to Galway County Council. Before his appointment as manager in Wexford, he worked as county accountant, county secretary, and assistant county manager with Limerick County Council. In 1964 he took first place and the gold medal in public administration from the Institute of Public Administration. He is also a fellow of the Chartered Institute of Secretaries and Administrators (FCIS).

Noel Dillon brought his own values, ambitions and beliefs to the job of Wexford County Manager and from them evolved the philosophy that underlay his approach to the many problems of administering a county such as Wexford. From the outset he outlined his aims and objectives which included community involvement, environmental awareness, urban renewal and a caring, innovative

The council's first purpose built public library at Barrack Lane, New Ross, opened in 1981.

Scarawalsh bridge, opened October 1976.

Thatcher at work, Kilmore 1989. In 1988 Wexford County Council initiated a grant scheme to assist owners of thatched cottages to maintain their property.

Rafter Bridge at Enniscorthy, opened 1991.

administration. Under his administration Wexford took the inaugural Environment Award in 1981 and received many awards for its urban renewal schemes. He also spearheaded the Redmond Square and Westgate developments in Wexford town and was instrumental in the development of the Irish National Heritage Park at Ferrycarrig. The refurbishment of the county hall and the provision of a new library headquarters and branch in Abbey Street, Wexford, were also among his initiatives.

He realised that his ideas and goals needed to be sold to have a chance of success and that public goodwill was vital. Public relations, therefore, was an important tool in winning support from the community and one he used fully to enhance the reputation of the council by showing the quality and variety of its services. In his seventeen years as manager, Noel Dillon became a conspicuous part of County Wexford: his work, his leisure and his family were all centred in the county.

Amenity block at Traveller halting site, New Ross, April 1989

In April 1993 he left Wexford to take up duty as manager in his home county of Cork, a position from which he is now retired. However, retirement has not ended his contribution to public service. Apart from his engagement as a lecturer in public administration at University College Cork, Noel Dillon is also chairman of An Chomhairle Leabharlanna (the Library Council); Director of the National Building Agency; a member of the interim board of the Ordnance Survey and a member of the Irish Government Devolution Commission. Formerly a member of the Environmental Council, the Environmental Awareness Bureau and the National Committee for European Year of the Environment, he is currently a member of the Advisory Committee to the Environmental Protection Agency. He continues his association with County Wexford as president of Comóradh '98.

Seamus Dooley

When Seamus Dooley was appointed Wexford County Manager in September 1993, he became only the fourth holder of the office since the establishment of the county management system in the early 1940s. He came to the position with a wealth of experience and an impressive record of achievement. Starting his career with Galway County Council, he travelled a well-recognised route to the top of his professional career, serving as town clerk in Macroom, Tipperary, Youghal and Athlone, county accountant in Leitrim, a period of ten years in Kerry during the 1980s as county secretary immediately prior to coming to Wexford as assistant county manager in 1989. He became county manager in Donegal in 1992 but his stay in the northwest was to last only eighteen months before he returned to Slaneyside to fill the vacancy created by the departure of Noel Dillon to Cork.

With his prior knowledge of the county, Seamus settled in quickly and during his stewardship he has overseen the progressive development of the county. His energetic leadership and proactive approach to management has contributed to the achievement of a broad range of council policies and objectives. In particular he has overseen the following projects:

- ISO 9002 Quality Award for Motor Taxation department
- redevelopment of the Irish National Heritage Park
- provision of the National 1798 Visitor Centre
- urban renewal programmes in Enniscorthy and Wexford and a seaside designation scheme in Courtown
- development of Kilmore Quay fishing port and leisure marina
- major infrastructure projects relating to roads, water and sewerage schemes to meet the development needs of the county.

Enniscorthy public library was officially opened on 24 January 1994.

The Bridge to Democracy at the National 1798 Visitor Centre, Enniscorthy.

Seamus is an ardent believer in providing for local community needs through the leadership of democratically elected local government agencies. He sees the strategies and initiatives in the government reform proposals, *Better Local Government – A Programme for Change*, as offering further opportunities to embrace participative democracy in the community for the greater benefit of all our citizens. *The Task Force on Integration of Local Government and Local Development Systems Report* will, in his view, be central to the successful implementation of the *Better Local Government* strategy.

He believes that the success of the council is achieved through the dedication of the elected members and the efforts of the staff and he has invested heavily in team building and developing consensus political decision-making to ensure effective and efficient organisational performance. His belief in the partnership model approach to interaction with the community and other agencies has been acknowledged. He contributed to the establishment of the County Wexford Forum (the predecessor of the County Strategy Group) which he chaired, and subsequently he has chaired the County Strategy Group. He has chaired the Wexford County Enterprise Board since its foundation and was a central figure in Comóradh '98, which was set up to commemorate the 1798 rebellion. Comóradh '98 was an excellent example of a partnership group, representative of the community and local authorities in the county, and owed much of its success in co-ordinating the 1798 bicentennial commemoration to the drive and personal commitment of Seamus Dooley.

County council recycling storage bays at Killurin landfill site.

He is committed to developing partnership solutions to all efforts to further the economic well-being of the county. Working with the tourism interests and the community, he supported the establishment of a new agency, County Wexford Tourism, to market and promote the county in a focused way. He is currently co-ordinating the preparation of a new strategy for the economic development of the county.

Despite his busy and full work schedule, he has also found time to participate in developing national policy on local government matters. He has served on commissions established by the Minister for the Environment and Local Government, including the commission on town local government which produced the report entitled *Towards Cohesive Local Government – Town and County*, the Register of Electors review body, the national Travellers Consultative Group and the EPA advisory group dealing with the formulation of the national hazardous waste management plan.

He holds a diploma in arbitration and certificates in public relations and management from the Open University. He regards the management of change as a constant challenge, to ensure that the council can respond to the needs of the community, and he is looking forward enthusiastically to the work of adapting the council to meet the challenges of our society in the twenty-first century.

LIST OF COUNTY MANAGERS AND OTHER OFFICERS

County Managers

The County Management Act 1940 came into effect on 26 August 1942. The first Wexford county manager was appointed by the Minister for Local Government from that day. The holders of the office of county manager to date have been:

Thomas D Sinnott, 26 August 1942 - 31 October 1953
Thomas F Broe, 1 June 1954 - 31 May 1976
Michael Noel Dillon, 1 June 1976 - 12 April 1993
James Dooley, 1 September 1993-

Assistant County Managers

Patrick Whelan, 1 October 1979 - 21 March 1983
John Quinlivan, 5 December 1983 - 7 February 1988
James Dooley, 4 September 1989 - 5 April 1992
John Hutchinson, 5 January 1993 -

Special Developments Manager

Francis Adrian Doyle, 1 January 1998 -

County Surveyors and County Engineers

Henry Webster, 22 April 1899 - 30 June 1909
Stafford Gaffney, 1 July 1909 - 31 January 1912
William F Barry, 1 February 1912 - 1 December 1942
T Kelly, 1 June 1944 - 31 October 1945
Joseph Doris, 18 November 1946 - 4 April 1961
Donal Kavanagh, 1 April 1962 - 31 August 1968
Joseph O'Connor, 1 January 1970 - 31 December 1976
Gerard M Forde, 1 January 1977 - 31 March 1983
Philip Callery, 1 January 1986 -

County Secretaries

Capt. W H S Piggott, 22 April 1899 - January 1906
N J Frizelle, 26 February 1906 - 12 May 1944
George Cannon, 1 March 1945 - 30 June 1947
Tomás P Mac Diarmada, 1 June 1948 - 31 January 1957
Patrick O'Halloran, 1 October 1957 - 22 October 1959
Séamus Ó Gallchóbair, 1 November 1960 - 25 February 1969
William P Creedon, 1 May 1970 - 12 February 1995
Francis Adrian Doyle, 12 July 1995 - 31 December 1997
John J Pierce, 12 January 1998 -

MANAGEMENT TEAM
Seated, L to R:
John Pierce, Co. Secretary;
Seamus Dooley, Co. Manager;
Phil Callery, Co. Engineer.
Standing, L to R:
Adrian Doyle,
Special Developments Manager,
Kieran O'Brien, Finance Officer;
John Hutchinson, Asst Co. Manager.

Bicycles on cement stands in the front building of County Hall were a familiar sight in the 1950s and 60s.

Working for the Council

IN THE EARLY YEARS OF ITS EXISTENCE, Wexford County Council employed few administrative staff. The responsibility for implementing the decisions and policies of the elected members fell to the council's senior officials, the county surveyor and secretary who were given a discretionary allowance to employ clerical assistants privately. These clerical assistants were usually male and were required to be qualified in both shorthand and typing and to have a knowledge of the Irish language. From time to time the council itself would employ one of these clerks in a more permanent capacity. For example, in August 1911 the council considered applications for the position of stenographer and typist. In his letter of application the successful candidate, a Mr James H Cadogan, wrote:

> I enclose a reference from Mr Frizelle [county secretary] as whose private Clerk I acted for four years and from which you will see my qualifications for the position. My shorthand speed is 175 words per minute, and typing speed 70 words per minute. I attach a certificate from Intermediate Commissioners showing I passed with honours in Irish at the examination in 1899.

Mr Cadogan was employed at a salary of £1 per week. In June 1908 the council staff

Workmen employed at Carrickfoyle quarry during the 1940s. L to R: John Carroll, Ballyhitt (ganger); Paddy Murphy, Rowestown; Tom Sweeney, Keelogues; Miley Caulfield, Park (carter); Brendan Carroll (ganger, later foreman).

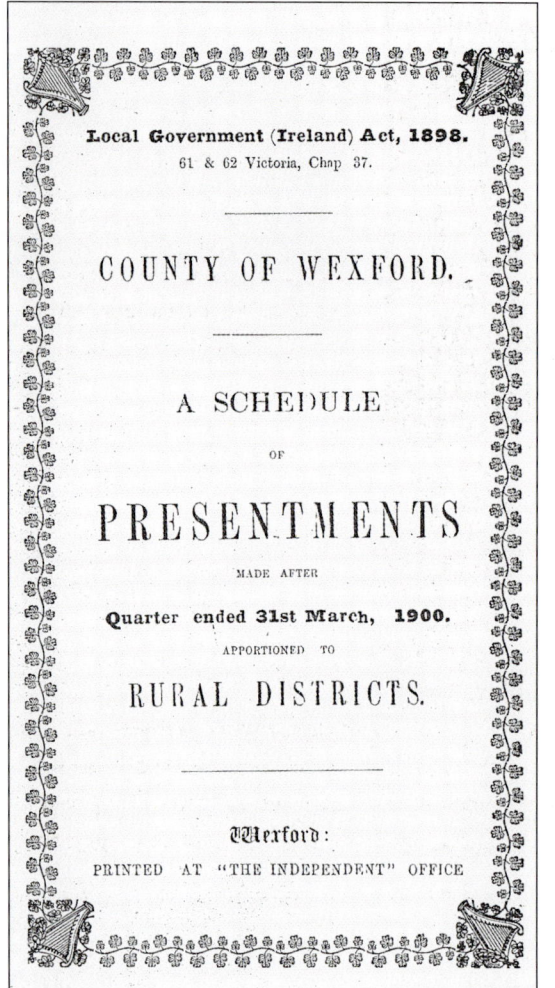

Extract from list of road contracts for New Ross No 1 district, covering the period 31 July 1900 to 30 June 1905.

The system of presentments continued into the early years of the council.

Work crew at Carrickfoyle quarry during the 1940s. L to R: Patrick Breen, Kingsford (labourer); John Wickham, Ballindinas (labourer); David Rossiter, Glenduff, Barntown; Michael Connick, Bargy Commons (time keeper); James Kehoe, Greenlake, Murrintown (labourer); Michael Goodison, Ballyhine (labourer).

Council workers laying concrete road outside Kelly's Hotel, Rosslare, c.1930.

were granted holidays as follows: county surveyor, one month; county secretary, three weeks; clerical staff, two weeks, 'to be taken as the exigencies of official work permit'.

Until the early 1920s, the council continued the practice of its predecessor, the grand jury, of building and maintaining roads and bridges by contracting the work to local farmers and landowners. However, after World War I, agitation by

A stone crusher of the type used by the council to prepare metalling for roads. It is seen here being driven by a steam engine at a rally in Tagoat, August 1997.

In the late 1920s and early '30s the council began to use concrete as a road surface. Picture shows a stretch of Enniscorthy concrete road still extant in May 1970.

unemployed men against this practice persuaded the council to change its policy and to employ labourers directly on repair and maintenance work. This led to conflict with the farming community who complained that farm labourers were being lured away from farming by the prospect of a better paying job with the council. The opening of additional council quarries in the 1920s provided further work opportunities for labourers. At first, quarry workers were employed on a piecework basis, hand-breaking rocks for 9d (about 4p) per ton. By the early 1930s, however, quarry labourers were being organised into work gangs and were employed at an hourly rate. The job of carting the stone was frequently contracted to local farmers who could provide their own horses and carts.

The council also elected a number of persons to collect its revenue. Every rate collector was required to be bonded by providing the council with the names of a number of individuals willing to act as his or her guarantors. The rate collectors submitted their account books annually to be 'written up' and they lodged the collected revenue with the council's treasurer, the National Bank. Frequently, the council found it necessary to take on additional temporary clerical staff to 'write up' the rate books. During the War of Independence and the Civil War, the rate collectors often found themselves targeted by both sides. Some complained to the council that their houses had been raided by the military or by 'armed and masked men' and their account books and money confiscated. Others resigned, saying they feared for their lives if they continued as agents of the council. Clerical and administrative staff also faced disruption during this period. The council offices were frequently raided by the military and ledgers and documents confiscated. Further upheaval was caused when the council was forced out of County Hall and its offices temporarily located first in a disused ward of the workhouse, then in

Some members of the council staff, c. 1947. L to R: Peggy O'Connor, Bridie Doyle, Sean Dunbar, Kathleen Sinnott, Lorcan Kiernan, Eileen Hearne, Ursula Kelly, Margaret Mitchell, Allie Walsh, Maura O'Rafferty, Peggy Doyle, Mal Donohoe.

Wexford's town hall and finally and more permanently in Fortview, a residence on Spawell Road just opposite County Hall. The council's headquarters and offices remained at Fortview until 1931.

During the 1920s, as council services began to expand, the number of clerical and administrative staff directly employed by the council began to rise. When the rural district councils were abolished in 1925, their clerks were absorbed into the county council staff. The establishment of the Local Appointments Commission in 1926 effectively took away the council's discretion in recruitment to its senior administrative and professional posts. As these positions had now to be advertised nationally, it became less likely that they would be filled by local candidates. By the 1930s more women were being employed, mainly as shorthand typists. However, women had few promotional prospects unless they chose to remain single: until 1973 women were obliged to resign upon marriage.

The second world war necessarily curtailed the council's services and little recruitment took place. In August 1942, following the appointment of Wexford's first county manager, the Board of Health and Public Assistance was abolished and most of its administrative staff transferred to the council. The responsibility for employing staff now rested ultimately with the county manager. By the mid-1940s a recognisable staff grading structure had emerged. Each department had a staff officer supervising a number of clerical officers and clerk/typists. In the post-war period, as the council's services began to expand, a major recruitment drive was undertaken which brought many young people into the service. Among these new recruits were Kathleen Lucking, employed as library assistant in 1947, and Billy Ringwood who became a clerical officer in 1948. Their memories of their early years with the council form the basis of what follows.

By the late 1940s the county council was one of the principal 'white collar' employers in the county and there was keen competition for its clerical positions. Recruitment was through competitive examination and interview. The examination, which could be described as an 'easy' Leaving Certificate, took place over several days, usually in the council chamber. There were compulsory papers in Irish, English and mathematics: additional papers included history, geography and Latin. An oral Irish examination followed. Those with the highest marks in the examination were then interviewed by an independent board and the successful candidates duly appointed. The starting salary for a clerical officer/library assistant was £10 per month.

Although County Hall had been extensively renovated during the 1930s, its decor was still gloomily institutional. The interior walls were painted in dark colours and linoleum covered the floors and stairs. Council staff worked a five and a half day week, from Monday at 9 am to Saturday at 1 pm. The bicycle was the principal mode of transport to work because few staff could afford the luxury of a car. A line of bicycles on cement stands in the front building of County Hall became a familiar sight.

The new recruits were trained in by older, experienced members of staff, many of whom had served with the council since the 1920s. Billy Ringwood recalled the names of many of these long-serving staff members and the departments with which they were most associated, including: Sean O'Kennedy (Accounts); Denny Doran (General Purposes); Denny Radford (Roads); Bob Shortall (Home

Youthful exuberance at the local government dinner dance in the Talbot Hotel, Wexford, 14 December 1950. Among those identified are: Dympna Kiernan, Gwen Binions, Elsie Roche, Tom Dixon, Tom O'Connor, Angela Walsh, Con Dwyer, Betty Carty, Kathleen Roche, Thomas F Byrne, Mollie Lowney, Kitty Bolger, Eileen Kehoe, Billy Ringwood, Lila Doyle, Eileen Doyle, John O'Dwyer, Breda McDonald, Ned Magner, Doney O'Connor, Ursula Kelly, Mary Browne, Paddy Drury, Bridie Doyle, Mal Donohoe, Michael Cleary, Joan Hannon, Padge Kinsella, Jim Sinnott, Noel Doyle, Paddy Murphy, Bridie Rose Walsh, Tony Cronin, Allisha Murphy, Michael Murphy, Peggy Lucking, Kathleen Mullaly.

County council staff dance committee, November 1960.
Standing, L to R: Ger Leahy, Tony Cronin, Dr D Stokes, Paddy Murphy, Billy Ringwood, Jack Carroll.
Seated, L to R: Mary Wall, Betty Doyle, Róisín O'Brien.

Assistance); Nicky Kehoe (Births, Deaths and Marriages); Nicky Beary (Rates); 'Jackers' Maloney (Accounts, Chief Clerk); Nora Connolly (Library); Tommy Brown (General Purposes and Roads) and Mal Donohoe (Motor Tax). Communication between senior and junior staff was quite formal. The use of first names was rare and staff were usually addressed as Mister X or Miss Y. An intercom was used for communications between offices. However, this instrument was not always used for the purpose for which it was intended. One individual, whose talent for imitating the voices of senior officials became legendary, occasionally used the intercom to summon a colleague to the manager's or the secretary's office on an entirely fictitious errand, with predictable consequences.

Owing to the fact that the council embarked on major road and house-building schemes during the 1950s, the number of directly-employed workmen rose significantly. By the mid-1950s the council was employing almost 700 men on road construction and maintenance. It also had a team of masons, carpenters and labourers employed in building new cottages and in maintaining and repairing the 4,000 or so council cottages already in existence.

The social life of the staff improved enormously with the formation in 1950 of the council Social Club. Its primary purpose was to raise money for the annual staff dress dance which became a feature of staff life in the 1950s and 60s. The large number of young men and women working together inevitably produced office romances and many of these blossomed into marriage. In 1961 the council staff entered the local Tops of the Town competition for the first time. It continued its participation until 1981, winning the local competition six times during that period. In 1976 the council Tops team came third in the national competition and it was placed fifth in Ireland in 1981.

Following the formation of the health boards in 1971, several departments, including Health and Home Assistance and Registration of Births, Deaths and

Marriages, which had previously been the responsibility of the county council, transferred to the South Eastern Health Board. As some departments left County Hall, new ones were formed. In the early 1970s the innovative County Development Team, based in County Hall, brought council staff into direct and co-operative contact with the local business and industrial sectors. Over the years the work engaged in by council staff has become diversified. There are now over 700 people employed by the council throughout the county. Apart from the traditional work of the council, the staff are now actively involved in promoting tourism, creating awareness of and encouraging enterprise activity, monitoring pollution, raising public awareness of environmental issues, acting as civil defence volunteers, facilitating arts and culture projects, and providing training in information technology.

Staff photograph taken in 1968. Front row, L to R: Mary La Roche, Aileen O'Keefe, Anita La Roche, Marie McGee, Maura Forde, Ann O'Byrne, Betty Doran, Betty Stamp, Bridie Moran, Ann Power, Philomena Roche, Nuala Doyle, Margaret O'Neill, Carmel Kehoe, Nellie Hore, Mary Wall. Second row, L to R: Maureen Fortune, Carol O'Reilly, Maura Miskella, Peter McQuillan, Dick Phelan, George Furlong, Mary Sheridan, Anna Drury, Jack Carroll, Mal Donohoe, Tony Cronin, Paddy Byrne, Maurice Flynn, Ger Leahy, Dave Broderick.

Third row, L to R: Mary Jones, Anna May Tyrell, Imelda Byrne, Joan Meyler, Eithne Donnelly, Maura Butler, Imelda Byrne, Sheila Breen, Elva Cardiff, Stella Quirke, Gretta McCarthy, Mai Keane, Ann O'Byrne, Esther Whelan, Nancy Woods. Fourth row, L to R: Mary O'Neill, Sean Dunbar, Brendan Barry, Michael Daly. Back row, L to R: Dan Duggan, Billy Ringwood, Gerard Kehoe, Dick Keane, Paddy Drury, Tom Cleary, Tony Murphy, T J Grant, Yens Other, Nick Cloke, Jackie Power, Lorcan Kiernan.

WORKING FOR THE COUNCIL

DEVELOPMENT OFFICE AND ARTS OFFICE
L to R: Dolores Whitty, Mary Cleere, Martin McDonald, Anita Rossiter, Lorraine Comer.

ENVIRONMENT AND SANITARY SERVICES
Seated, L to R: Ambrose Madders, Eddie Barrett, Claire O'Connor, Anne O'Reilly, Jackie Murphy, Darragh Cullinane.
Standing, L to R: Tim Murphy, Mark Collins, Karl Fagan, Jackie Power, Peadar McDonald, Eddie Redmond, Ian Plunkett, Paula Shortall, Liam Ruttledge, Nóirín Byrne, Ger O'Brien, Tony Shanley, Billy Byrne, Noel Stacey, Christine Chapman.

FINANCE SECTION

Seated, L to R: Martina Birney, Annette O'Neill, Marie Thorpe, Ann Doyle.
Standing, L to R: Lynda Lacey, Nora Cardiffe, Angela Kirwan, Denis Noonan, Angela Sutherland, Aidan Doyle, Pam Morris, Siobhán Kehoe.

HOUSING SECTION

Seated, L to R: Catríona O'Sullivan, Niall McDonnell, Ailish Foley, Fiona Wadding.
Standing, L to R: Eileen Wallace, Padraic McKenna, Anthony Nolan, Tracey Maguire, Michael Stafford, Tina O'Rourke.

WORKING FOR THE COUNCIL

HOUSING SECTION - DRAWING OFFICE
Seated, L to R: Niamh O'Connor, Donal McCarthy, Kevin Hurley.
Standing, L to R: John Roberts, Leonard Poole, Eamon Nash.

HOUSING AND LOANS AND GRANTS SECTIONS
Seated, L to R: Mae Keane, Hugh Maguire.
Standing, L to R: Susan Ffrench, Caroline Kennedy.

I.T. SECTION
Seated, L to R: Marina O'Byrne, Patricia Foley, Siobhán Redmond.
Standing, L to R: Margot Murphy, Caroline Healy, Catherine Kavanagh, Ger Griffin, P J Murphy, Rita Byrne, Elizabeth Gordon, Peter O'Connor, Jane Duignan, Margaret Corish.

LIBRARY SECTION
Seated, L to R: Jarlath Glynn, Kathy Frayne.
Standing, L to R: Gerardette Roche, Sean Furlong, Vincent Byrne, Angie Parle, Michael Dempsey, Joan Lambert, Rita O'Brien, Celestine Rafferty, Anne Griffin.

MOTOR TAX SECTION
Seated, L to R: Sharon Furlong, Siobhán Wheeler, Anne Sullivan, Anne Walsh, Mary Cowman.
Standing, L to R: Tricia O'Shea, Mary Coleman, Emma Fitzgerald, Maureen Roche, Susan Doran, Teresa Codd, Ray Colfer, Alice O'Gorman, Cian Meachair, Tara Farrell, Anne Sinnott.

PERSONNEL SECTION (1)
Back, L to R: Grace Nolan, Stephanie Furlong, Catherine Kirby, Laura Williams, Phyl Healy, Pat Devereux, Caroline O'Mara. Front, L to R: Debbie Roice, Karen Moore, Tony Larkin, Geraldine Cullen, Liz Coughlan.

PERSONNEL SECTION (2)
Seated, L to R: Catherine White, Esther Lannay, Janice Jordan.
Standing, L to R: Assumpta Doyle, Michael O'Reilly, Liz Stanley.

RATES SECTION
L to R: Jim Bell, Annette Malone, Joan Murphy, Edwina Colfer, Frances Stafford.

PLANNING

Seated, L to R: David Bowen, Dympna Shanahan, Benny Sullivan, Diane Roche, Clem Daly.

Standing, L to R: Andrew Spencer, Kevin Redmond, David Minogue, Breda Quigley, Martin Ryan, Suzanne Brennan, Dan O'Donovan, Mary Grier, Kevin Kehoe, Monica Gaynor, Michelle Browne, Helen O'Mahoney, T J Mahoney, Anne White, Clair Walsh.

ROADS SECTION, FIRE SECTION AND CIVIL DEFENCE

Seated, L to R: Claire Redmond, Marguerite McGrath, Anita Ryan, Maria Farrell, Bernie Doyle.

Standing, L to R: Gabrielle Willis, Jim Staples, David Kennedy, Niall McGuigan, Paul Wilson, Sean McDermott, Helen Frayne.

WORKING FOR THE COUNCIL

REVENUE COLLECTORS
Seated, L to R: Billy Myers, Thomas Cullimore, Sarah O'Neill, Michael Breen. Standing, L to R: John McCormack, Brian Dunphy, Billy Courtney, Martin Hickey, Michael Stamp, Thomas Boggan, Jim Doran.

WEXFORD AREA OFFICE
Front Row, L to R: Dick Donoghue, Jim Power, Geraldine Reck, Noeleen Troy, Patrick Monaghan, Andy Monaghan, Tom Byrne, Christy Murphy. Middle Row, L to R: Michael Fitzgerald, Richard Martin, Joe Busher, Jimmy Daly, Tony Murphy, Mark Redmond. Back Row, L to R: James Monaghan, Gerry Forde, Nicky Walsh, Johnny Bolger, Ned Flood, Marks Hogan.

WEXFORD FIREFIGHTERS

Front, L to R: Michael Roche, Brendan Smith, Bernard Gavin, Pat Doyle, P J Doran, Dermot Cunningham.

Back, L to R: Declan Cunningham, Tony Godkin, Kieran Scallan, David Lloyd, Kevin Breen.

CLEANING STAFF

L to R: Janice Jordan, Winnie Ennis, Peggy Walsh, Imelda Malone, Marie Murphy, Doris Byrne.

MACHINERY YARD, ENNISCORTHY

Seated, L to R: Mary Kehoe, Catherine Coade, John Dunne.

Standing, L to R: Bernard Dunne, Michael Pierce, Pat Roche, Dan Conroy.

WORKING FOR THE COUNCIL

BUNCLODY FIREFIGHTERS
Left to right: Tom Roche, John Melay, Patsy Cowman, Patrick Cowman, Martin Byrne (in the cab).

ENNISCORTHY AREA OFFICE
Front, L to R: John Flynn, Eamonn Hore, Joe Moorehouse, John McGrath, John Murphy, Peter Reck.
Middle, L to R: Paul O'Brien, James Rattigan, Colm Quirke, M J Rossiter, Larry Cloke, Pat Hendrick, John Redmond.
Back, L to R: Michael Murphy, John Furlong, Larry Mitten, Fran Breen, Michael Sinnott, Pat Cloke, Pat Cowman.

ENNISCORTHY FIREFIGHTERS
Left to right: Warren Mitten, Barry O'Brien, Aidan Wildes, Billy Dobbs, Patrick Murphy, Anthony Nolan, Danny O'Connor, Chris Wildes, Denis Doyle, Pat O'Connor.

GOREY AREA OFFICE (1)
Front, L to R: Thomas Carter, Jim Moore, Tony Levingstone, Bertie Cousins, Peter Tobin, Jim McDonald.
Standing, L to R: Dan Carroll, Tom Smith, Eddie Carter, Jack Tomkins, Michael Redmond, Tom Doyle, Tom Byrne.

WORKING FOR THE COUNCIL

GOREY AREA OFFICE (2)
Seated: Lillian McDonald.
Standing: Tina O'Sullivan.

GOREY FIREFIGHTERS
Left to right:
Keith Davis,
Anthony O'Hara,
Albert Willoughby,
Joe Dixon,
Richard Millar,
John Murphy,
Romano Duggan,
Owen Kennedy,
Billy Duncan,
Kevin Rossiter.

NEW ROSS AREA OFFICE
Seated, L to R: Frank Roche, George Walsh, Mairin Ralph, Breda Bolger, Johnny Gray. Standing, L to R: Joe O'Dwyer, Paddy Moore, Martin Doyle, John Franklin, Martin Shalloe, Michael J. Aspel, Martin Wickham, Charlie Rochford.

NEW ROSS FIREFIGHTERS
Left to right: Sylvester McGarr, Eddie Haberlin, Johnny Caulfield, Len Warren, Cyril McGarr, Maurice Caulfield, John Doyle, Richard Pyne.

COUNTY COUNCIL STAFF AT 31 DECEMBER 1998

Management Team

County Manager	Seamus Dooley
Assistant County Manager	John Hutchinson
County Engineer	Phil Callery
County Secretary	John Pierce
Finance Officer	Kieran O'Brien
Special Developments Manager	Adrian Doyle

Administrative/Clerical Grades

Administrative Officers	Niall McDonnell
	Tony Larkin
	David Minogue
	Anne O'Reilly
	Ger Griffin
Freedom of Information Officer	Assumpta Doyle
Senior Staff Officers	P J Murphy
	Assumpta Doyle
	Hugh Maguire
	Maeve O'Brien
	Ann Walsh
	Annette O'Neill
Staff Officers	Jim Bell
	Michael O'Reilly
	Martin McDonald
	Martina Donoghue
	Noel Stacey
	Rita Byrne
	Jacqueline Eydt
	Martina Bierney
	Catherine Kavanagh
	Dympna Shanahan
Assistant Staff Officers	Marina O'Byrne
	Emma Fitzgerald
	Peadar McDonald
	Caroline Kennedy
	Nóirín Byrne
	Alice Doyle
	Ann Sullivan
	Caroline O'Mara
	Anita Ryan
	Adrienne Larkin
	Elizabeth Stanley

Clerical Officers	Mae Keane
	Noeline Troy
	Diana Roche
	Mary Prendergast
	Angela Maguire
	Mary O'Leary
	Katherine Dempsey
	Mary Cleere
	Ray Colfer
	Peter Reck
	Mary Bowie
	Máirín Ralph
	Maureen Roche
	Patricia Devereux
	Anthony Nolan
	Mary Kehoe
	Catherine Coade
	Margaret O'Brien
	Jackie Murphy
	Marie Thorpe
	Bob Cowman
	Patricia Foley
	Pam Morris
	Helen Frayne
	Breda Bolger
	Patricia O'Shea
	Siobhán Kehoe
	Lillian McDonald
	Deborah Roice
	Mary Kehoe
	Tina O'Rourke
	Tina O'Sullivan
	Monica Hayes
	Alice O'Gorman
	Denis Noonan
	Nora Connor
	Margaret Geoghegan
	Dolores Whitty
	Lynda Lacey
	Mary Cowman
	Siobhán Wheeler
	Catherine Kirby
	Jane Duignan
	Anita Rossiter

Administrative/Clerical Grades (cont.)

		Revenue Collectors	Michael Stamp
			Thomas Cullimore
	Michelle Browne		Nicholas Scallan
	Claire O'Connor		William Myers
	Breda Quigley		John McCormack
	Margaret Corish		Martin Hickey
	Geraldine Reck		Thomas Boggan
	Nora Cardiff		Michael Breen
	Kathy Frayne		Mairéad Kavanagh
	Fiona Wadding	*Area Housing Officers*	Ger Mackey
	Laura Williams		Joe Curran
	Anne White		Padraig McKenna
	Ann Marie Devlin		Michael Stafford
	Annette Malone	*Storekeeper*	John Dunne
	Helen O'Mahoney	*Social Workers*	Dolores Traynor
	Bernie Doyle		Eileen Wallace
	Phyl Healy	*Senior Executive Engineers*	Tom Fahy
	Bridget Kelly		Niall McGuigan
	Mary Carton		Daragh Cullinane
	Maria Farrell	*County Architect*	Donal McCarthy
	Tara Farrell	*Chief Fire Officer*	Sean McDermott
	Paula Shortall	*Senior Executive Planning*	Ros Nixon
	Catríona O'Sullivan	*Executive Engineers*	Paul Wilson
	Elizabeth Gibbons		Frank Roche
	Christine Chapman		Ambrose Madders
	Siobhán Redmond		Paddy Ryan
	Geraldine Cullen		Clem Daly
	Bridget Breen		George Walsh
	Angela Murphy		Noel O'Driscoll
	Siobhán Carthy		Eamonn Hore
Local Government Auditor	Liam Bowe		Jim Power
Arts Officer	Lorraine Comer		Dan O'Donovan
Co. Librarian	Fionnuala Hanrahan		Gerry Forde
Assistant Librarians	Jarlath Glynn	*Assistant Chief Fire Officer*	Dave Kennedy
	Rita O'Brien	*Executive Planners*	Kevin Redmond
Senior Library Assistants	Celestine Rafferty		David Bowen
	Angela Parle	*Assistant Fire Officer*	Tadhg O'Shea
	Anne Griffin	*Assistant Engineer*	Laurence Foley
Library Assistants	Gerardette Roche	*Executive Technicians*	Mick Daly
	Theresa Goggin		John Cronin
	Vincent Byrne	*Technicians Grade I*	Nick Cloke
	Michael Dempsey		Liam Ruttledge
Branch Librarians	Lucy Wall-Murphy		Eddie Redmond
	Kathleen Gleeson	*Environmental Tech. Grade I*	James Rattigan
Library Mobile Driver	Sean Furlong	*Architectural Tech. Grade II*	Kevin Hurley
Library Porter/Driver	John Hall	*Environmental Tech. Grade II*	Eddie Bolger

Civil Technicians Grade II

Clerks of Works

Technical Services Supervisor
Technical Assistant
Veterinary Officer
Civil Defence Officer
Offset Machine Operator
Telephonist
Programmer
Dog Control Warden

Jim Staples
Kevin Kehoe
Tim McGrath
Shem Byrne
Philip Wallace
Benny Sullivan
Edward J Nash
John Roberts
Daniel Conroy
Michael Pierce
Jackie Power
Larry Forristal
Gabrielle Willis
Elizabeth Coughlan
Richard Phelan
Peter O'Connor
James Mulhall

County Wexford Firefighters

Wexford area

Bernard Gavin
Station Officer
Pat Doyle
A/Station Sub Officer
Michael Roche
Ciaran Scallan
Pat Doyle
David Lloyd
Dermot Cunningham
Declan Cunningham
Brendan Smith
Thomas Farnan
Kevin Breen

Gorey area

Richard Millar
Station Officer
John Murphy
Sub Station Officer
Albert Willoughby
William Duncan
Liam Doyle
M J Kenny
Joe Dixon
Kevin Rossiter
Romano Duggan
Patrick O'Hara
Keith Davis

Bunclody area

Patrick Cowman
Station Officer
Martin Byrne
Sub Station Officer
Thomas Roche
John Masterson
Tony Black
John Melay

Enniscorthy area

Patrick Murphy
Station Officer
Billy Dobbs
Station Sub Officer
Patrick O'Connor
Aidan Wildes
Danny O'Connor
Denis Doyle
Joe Millar
Anthony Nolan
Chris Wildes
Joe Foley
Barry O'Brien
Warren Mitten

New Ross area

Cyril McGarr
Station Officer
Len Warren
Sub Station Officer
John Caulfield
Thomas Condon
Richard Pyne
John Doyle
Pat Laffan
Patrick O'Neill
Edward Haberlin
Maurice Caulfield
Sylvester McGarr

Machinery Yard, Enniscorthy

Myles Cullen	Tom Siggins	John Kelly
Tommy Cullen	Richard Doyle	Jim O'Brien
Billy Byrne	Tommy Doyle	Pat Quigley
Pat Roche	Seamus Fenlon	Jack Hanrahan
Joe Phillips	Larry Delaney	James Kavanagh
Michael Quigley	Myles Quigley	Matty Kehoe
Peter Byrne	Fred Carley	Tom Dagg
Pat Tyrell	Michael Delaney	Seamus O'Leary
Paddy Quinn	Liam Kirwan	Bernard Kirwan
Martin Nolan	James Doyle	Peter Dagg
Bernard Dunne	Dan Breen	Bill Murphy
Paidh Redmond	Pat O'Leary	Michael Dunbar
John Breen	Stephen Breen	Martin O'Connor
Pat Leacy	Christy Doyle	Andy Fenlon
Billy Buckley	Pat Kehoe	Tom Quigley
Larry Delaney Jnr	Seamus Davitt	

Wexford Area Office

Sean Ellard	Claire O'Halloran	Peter Kehoe
P J Breen Jnr	Stephen Moran	Bill Kearns
Andrew Monaghan	Thomas Goff	Eamonn O'Grady
Nicholas Morris	William Redmond	John Miller
Thomas Stanners	Sean Redmond	Myles Kehoe
Joseph Goff	Patrick Nacey	James Monaghan
John Sinnott	Gerard O'Reilly	Edward Flood
T Corish	Tony Murphy	Frank Bolger
Frank O'Grady	Gerard Doyle	Matthew Monaghan
Patrick Kavanagh	Joseph Donoghue	Dick Donohoe
Thomas Byrne	Michael Furlong	John Doyle
R Martin	James Daly	Christy Murphy
M Griffin	Joe Busher	Michael Fitzgerald
T J Grant	Thomas Hughes	John Usher
Brian Pask	Michael Carty	Michael Sutherland
Dan Donovan	Mark Redmond	G O'Reilly
M Hogan	Nicholas Walsh	Mervyn McManus
A Doyle	Patrick Carthy	James Redmond
Seamus Donohoe	Johnny Bolger	Stephen Foley
Thomas Horan	Patrick O'Gorman	Peter O'Connor
Thomas Goff Jnr	Brian Kehoe	John Devereux
Michael Higginbottom	Sean Murphy	P Monaghan
Patrick Howlin	Brian Kenny	Bernard Kirwan
S Breen		

Gorey Area Office

Daniel Grannell	Myles Byrne	Peter Jordan
William Phillips	Thomas Kavanagh	Daniel Carroll
Denis Kavanagh	Matthew Redmond	Thomas Doyle
Patrick Allen	Patrick Kavanagh	James Dunbar
James Kearney	John Tomkins	Noel Murphy
Peter Redmond Jnr	Patrick Byrne	Chris Davitt
James O'Brien	Edward Sheridan	James Kavanagh
Michael Redmond	Martin Tobin	James Kavanagh
Morgan O'Brien	Liam Dunne	Edward O'Connor
Paul Kehoe	James Dunbar	Bertie Cousins
Tommy Smith	Thomas Byrne	Marcus McDonald
John Kennedy	Thomas Murphy	Peter Allen
Francis Kehoe	Cecil Goff	Paul Goff
Johnny Lawlor	Michael Redmond	Ian McLoughlin
John Redmond	James Hall	Peter Tobin
Daniel Murphy	Andrew Redmond	Edward Carter
Thomas Carter	Basil Kennedy	John Kennedy
Philip O'Connor	Andrew Dempsey	Paul Murphy
Matthew Byrne	Jim Moore	Jim McDonald
Tony Levingstone	Thomas Crowe	

Enniscorthy Area Office

James Raleigh	Laurence Mitten	Vincent Byrne
Thomas Armstrong	Anthony Reddy	Oliver Kearns
Patrick Dunphy	John Aylward	Aidan Murphy
Michael Rossiter	Daniel Nolan	William Murphy
James Breslin	Thomas Larkin	William Kehoe
James Cooney	Philip Flynn	Seamus Davis
John Banville	Colm Quirke	Patrick Cloke
Michael Sinnott	Paul O'Brien	John Redmond
John Furlong	Patrick Armstrong	John Flynn
John Murphy	Thomas Hogan	Michael O'Neill
James Doyle	George Dunbar	Patrick Hendrick
Laurence Cloke	Patrick Walsh	Joseph Moorehouse
John Walsh	Thomas Dagg	Matthew Flynn
Patrick O'Toole	John McGrath	James McGannon
Peter Kehoe	Patrick Murphy	Bernard Kelly
Michael Reddy	Thomas Whelan	John Quigley
Michael Brooks	William Kinsella	Frank Rochford
Michael Murphy	Peter Byrne	Patrick Cowman

New Ross Area Office

Sean Murphy	Patrick O'Neill	Thomas Sweeney
Henry Rochford	James Franklin	Nicholas Eustace
Joseph Doyle	Michael Aspel	Joseph O'Dwyer
Patrick Kehoe	John Grey	John Hanley
John Howlett	Martin Doyle	William Murphy Jnr
William Kinsella	John Kehoe	Martin Connick
Thomas Nolan	John Dunne	Michael O'Grady
Martin Wickham	Martin Shalloe	John Sinnott
Brendan Molloy	Thomas Murphy	John Waters
Oliver Bennett	Dan McPhillips	Charles Rochford
Thomas Tobin	Mark O'Hanlon	Patrick Murphy
Michael Butler	Thomas Curran	Anne Chapman
Joseph Bradley Jnr	Patrick Moore	John Walsh
Thomas O'Neill	Patrick Dunne	John Franklin
Daniel Doyle	John Fardy	Seamus Walsh
John Cloney	James Barnwell	Edward Shalloe
Patrick Banville	Robert Bolger	Pat O'Neill
James Howlett	Sean Colfer	Mark Butler
James White	Philip French	Matt Ryan
Declan Rattigan	Tony Feeney	Gerard Roche
Ciaran Cullen		

Caretakers

Mary Nolan	John Kennedy	Daniel Kennedy
Thomas Carter	Nicholoas Cullen	Michael Reck
James Doyle	Patrick O'Toole	Catherine Masterson
Kathleen Thorpe	Michael Redmond	Patrick Rellis

FORMER EMPLOYEES

The achievements of the county council have relied extensively on the workers who implemented the schemes, policies and programmes from year to year. In the one hundred years of its existence the council has employed thousands of men and women. In the nature of things, many have, by now, passed away. While it would not be possible to name them all, their contribution to the public good is remembered and acknowledged.

Amongst the surviving former employees are:

Name	Location	Role
Paschal Whitmore	Wexford	Senior Staff Officer
Patrick Quigley	Caim	Revenue Collector
James Murray	New Ross	General Operative
P Redmond	Ballycanew	General Operative
Matthew Butler	Gorey	General Operative
Thomas Doyle	Killinick	Ganger
James Kehoe	Enniscorthy	Foreman
Michael Curran	Ballygarrett	Foreman
William Kinsella	Blackwater	General Operative
Kathleen Tobin	Enniscorthy	Clerical Officer
Thomas Leacy	New Ross	General Operative
Thomas Furlong	Taghmon	Craftsman
John McLoughlin	Cleariestown	General Operative
James Dooley	Blackwater	General Operative
Martin Murphy	Craanford	Craftsman
Thomas Kehoe	Clonroche	General Operative
Michael Shiggins	Oylegate	Chargehand
Walter Madigan	New Ross	Ganger
Timothy Larkin	Clonroche	Ganger
Martin O'Loughlin	Courtown	Rate Collector
Cecelia Kenny	Gorey	Rate Collector
Myles Underwood	Duncormick	Chargehand
David Moran	Killurin	General Operative
Art C Ward	New Ross	Assistant County Engineer
Thomas Ryan	Wexford	General Operative
James Furlong	Duncormick	General Operative
Thomas Murphy	Enniscorthy	General Operative
Thomas J McNulty	Gorey	Executive Engineer
Michael Bolger	Wexford	Craftsman
Thomas McCarthy	Ballycogley	Machinery Operative
Peter Sheil	Duncormick	Foreman
Owen Levingstone	Ferns	General Operative
Kevin Walsh	Duncormick	General Operative
James Lawless	Camolin	Handyman
Peter Gaynor	Taghmon	General Operative
William Doyle	Ferns	General Operative
Thomas Browne	Wexford	Staff Officer
William Coady	Kilmuckridge	Craftsman
Malachy Grace	Duncormick	General Operative
John Culleton	Kilmore	General Operative
Joseph Barton	Saltmills	General Operative
Patrick Bolger	Ballygarrett	General Operative
Denis McDonald	Craanford	Ganger
Philip O'Brien	Taghmon	Ganger
Michael Quigley	Barntown	Craftsman
Sean Monaghan	Duncormick	Chargehand
James P Colfer	Duncormick	Craftsman
Matthew Coady	Enniscorthy	Machinery Operative
William Murphy	Crossabeg	Craftsman's Mate
John Donohoe	Ballyhogue	Ganger
Patrick Clear	Bunclody	Ganger
Thomas Turner	Ferns	General Operative
Michael Whelan	Camolin	General Operative
John Ryan	New Ross	General Operative
Thomas Kearns	Ballyhogue	Machinery Operative
Thomas Colgan	Enniscorthy	Machinery Operative
Peter Ryan	Gorey	General Operative
Matthew O'Toole	Killanne	Machinery Operative
Thomas Kelly	Killinick	General Operative
Thomas Smyth	Hollyfort	General Operative
Art McDonald	Gorey	Overseer
Mark Fitzhenry	Kiltealy	Supervising Overseer
John Kinsella	Ballycanew	General Operative
Seamus Murphy	Enniscorthy	Technical Services Supervisor
William O'Connor	Oulart	Ganger
Patrick O'Neill	Ferns	Overseer
Thomas Molloy	Adamstown	General Operative
Patrick Cleary	Foulksmills	General Operative
John Duffy	Enniscorthy	Assistant Foreman (Craft)
James Kiely	Newbawn	Craftsman
Gerard M Forde	Wexford	County Engineer

Name	Location	Role
Denis F Byrne	Gorey	Rate Collector
Patrick Tyrell	Bunclody	Ganger
Thomas Quigley	Caim	Chargehand
Martin Foley	Ballycarney	Handyman
John Kavanagh	Ballycarney	Foreman
Patrick Turner	Ferns	General Operative
Betty Carty	Wexford	Clerical Officer
Alexander Crosbie	Adamstown	Foreman
James Levingstone	Ferns	Handyman
Murthe Deathe	Gorey	Ganger
Thomas O'Connor	Gorey	Clerical Officer
Michael Maher	Kilrane	General Operative
James Doyle	Ballygarrett	General Operative
Walter Byrne	Camolin	General Operative
Hugh O'Neill	Enniscorthy	Craftsman
John Nolan	Ballycarney	Ganger
Patrick O'Connor	Carnew	Rate Collector
Patrick Butler	Clonroche	Rate Collector
John Howlin	Bridgetown	Rate Collector
Garry Redmond	Enniscorthy	Rate Collector
Laurence Fitzharris	Ballycullane	Rate Collector
William Furlong	Campile	Rate Collector
Patrick O'Toole	Blackwater	Foreman
William Cooper	Caim	General Operative
Bridie Doyle	Wexford	Staff Officer
Michael Colfer	Bannow	General Operative
Richard Grant	Wexford	Foreman (Craft)
Laurence Butler	Gorey	Craftsman's Mate
Sean Quigley	Screen	Machinery Operative
John Whelan	Ballygarrett	Ganger
Mogue Lawless	Enniscorthy	Machinery Operative
Pierce Murphy	Enniscorthy	Revenue Collector
Thomas Murphy	Ferns	General Operative
Kevin Quinlan	Enniscorthy	Executive Engineer
Sean McLoughlin	Wexford	Senior Staff Officer
Ken Scanlon	Wexford	Clerk of Works
John Carroll	Wexford	Clerical Officer
James Barron	Ramsgrange	General Operative
Michael Nash	Taghmon	Craftsman
John Bass	Gorey	General Operative
Thomas Donohoe	Ballyhogue	Ganger
Thomas Cullen	Adamstown	Handyman
John O'Reilly	Wexford	General Operative
Edward Carroll	Barntown	General Operative
Thomas Murphy	Rathnure	Machinery Operative
Thomas Cogley	New Ross	Chargehand
Joseph Dowd	Barntown	Chargehand
Tim Harrington	Davidstown	Overseer
Kevin Foley	Clonroche	General Operative
Patrick Travers	Ballyhogue	Machinery Operative
Luke Whelan	Waterford	Craftsman
Arthur Murphy	Coolhull	Executive Engineer
James Thorpe	Enniscorthy	Draughtsman-Technician
Richard O'Neill	Killanne	Craftsman
John Jn Doyle	Wexford	Draughtsman-Technician
Michael Bennett	Co. Wexford	Foreman
William Kennedy	Clonroche	General Operative
Peter Walsh	New Ross	General Operative
Richard Purcell	Adamstown	Craftsman
Daniel Doyle	Enniscorthy	General Operative
Martin Ryan	Wexford	Draughtsman-Technician
Liam Browne	Enniscorthy	Craftsman
Philip Doyle	Ballygarrett	Overseer
Richard Murphy	Bunclody	Ganger
William Kennedy	Ferns	Ganger
Peter Wallace	Campile	General Operative
John Delaney	Foulksmills	General Operative
Patrick O'Connor	Oulart	General Operative
Patrick Morrissey	Enniscorthy	Ganger
Anthony Kehoe	Enniscorthy	General Operative
Samuel Walker	Gorey	Ganger
Michael Keegan	Wellingtonbridge	Chargehand
Joseph O'Rourke	Enniscorthy	Chargehand
Peter Breen	The Ballagh	General Operative
Michael Timmons	Ballygarrett	Ganger
Peter A Cronin	Wexford	Assistant Staff Officer
Arthur Sheridan	Gorey	Ganger
Joseph Burke	Ferns	Ganger
Daniel Duggan	Wexford	Senior Executive Engineer
Seamus Doyle	Ballymurn	General Operative
Matthew Cloke	Enniscorthy	Machinery Operative
Sean Dunbar	Ferrycarrig	Senior Staff Officer
Morgan O'Connor	Castlebridge	General Operative
Joseph Donohue	Curracloe	General Operative
John Atkinson	Ballindaggin	Craftsman
Matthew Byrne	Arklow	General Operative

James Savage	Oylegate	Overseer
John Foley	Fethard on Sea	Handyman
Patrick Stafford	Ramsgrange	General Operative
Laurence Shiggins	Castlebridge	Ganger
Neil Roche	Bridgetown	General Operative
James O'Leary	Wexford	Administrative Officer
Hugh O'Connor	The Ballagh	Ganger
Patrick Drury	Wexford	Staff Officer
Edward Doyle	Ballypreacus	Craftsman
Walter Rahilly	Wexford	Senior Executive Engineer
William Purcell	New Ross	Refuse Collector
Peter Coleman	Bunclody	Ganger
Thomas Moran	Tacumshane	Handyman
Michael Cooney	Bunclody	General Operative
Frank Carberry	Oylegate	General Operative
Edward O'Connor	Killenagh	Ganger
Thomas Rochford	Clonroche	Machinery Operative
Patrick Redmond	Screen	General Operative
Laurence O'Reilly	Camolin	Ganger
John Foley	Ferns	Ganger
James Walsh	Terrerath	Ganger
Nicholas Roche	Ballyhogue	General Operative
Patrick O'Brien	Ballyhogue	Chargehand
Francis Fanning	Colestown	Machinery Operative
Thomas Kinsella	Gorey	Ganger
Kathleen Lucking	Wexford	Assistant County Librarian
Michael Kinsella	Craanford	Handyman
William P Creedon	Wexford	County Secretary
Rose Walsh	Enniscorthy	Clerical Officer
Thomas Wickham	Duncormick	General Operative
Patrick Cullen	Inch	Ganger
William Ringwood	Wexford	County Development Officer
Thomas Murphy	Tagoat	General Operative
Kevin Campbell	Duncormick	Craftsman's Mate
Nicholas Morris	Killinick	General Operative
Peter McDonald	Gorey	Ganger
James McGee	Newbawn	Foreman
John Stafford	Taghmon	Ganger
Patrick Kehoe	Ballycullane	Ganger
Michael O'Grady	Ballycullane	Overseer
Patrick O'Toole	Kilmuckridge	Chargehand
Patrick Walshe	Rosslare Strand	Executive Engineer
Catherine O'Rourke	Wexford	County Librarian
Tom Lancaster	Clonroche	General Operative
John Deathe	Gorey	General Operative
Hubert McLoughlin	Oulart	Overseer
John Thorpe	Enniscorthy	Assistant Foreman (Craft)
Patrick Murphy	Ballymurn	Foreman
Patrick Scallan	Butlerstown	Chargehand
Nicholas Murphy	Enniscorthy	General Operative
Mark Morrissey	Moneytucker	Chargehand
James Gaynor	Barntown	Ganger
Thomas Carroll	Broadway	Chargehand
George Murphy	Curracloe	General Operative
James Dyce	Foulksmills	Chargehand
Leonard Stone	Barntown	General Operative
James Grant	Wexford	Craftsman
Joseph Bradley	Newbawn	Craftsman
James Kinsella	Gorey	General Operative
James Franklin	Adamstown	Gerneral Operative
Thomas O'Leary	Kiltealy	Gerneral Operative
James Doyle	Wexford	Draughtsman Technician
James Murphy	Blackwater	Craftsman
Francis Harewood	Galway	Chief Assistant County Engineer
Peter Kehoe	Ballycullane	Waterworks Caretaker
David Roche	Foulksmills	Craftsman
Noel Casey	Wexford	Senior Executive Engineer

Note: In a few cases the named grade is an equivalent title which may not accurately describe the precise nature of the employment. The council remains in contact with about one hundred widows and dependent children of former employees.

APPENDIX I

Council Elections and Schedules of Members 1899-1999

In November 1898 the Local Government Board fixed the number of county electoral divisions in County Wexford at eighteen, each returning one county councillor except Wexford Urban which was to return two. There were, therefore, nineteen directly elected members of the council. The chairmen of the four rural district councils were also ex officio members of the county council. Under section 3 of the Local Government (Ireland) Act 1898, the council was empowered to co-opt two additional members. The Act also permitted the grand jury to nominate three additional members to the first county council only. The total potential membership of the council was therefore twenty-eight in 1899 and twenty-five from 1902 onwards.

County Council Electoral Divisions 1899

District Electoral Divisions (DEDs)		District Electoral Divisions (DEDs)	
BALLYHUSKARD	Ardcavan, Ardcolm, Ballyhuskard, Castlellis, Kilmallock	MONOMOLIN	Ballyvaldon, Bolaboy, Castletalbot, Ford, Kilcormack, Killincooley, Monomolin, Wells
BANNOW	Ballymitty, Bannow, Clongeen, Duncormack, Harperstown, Harriestown, Horetown, Newbawn	NEW ROSS	New Ross Rural, New Ross Urban, Rosbercon Urban
BRIDGETOWN	Aughwilliam, Bridgetown, Kilcowan, Killag, Kilmore, Mayglass, Newcastle, Rathaspick	NEWTOWNBARRY	Ballybeg, Ballyellis, Castledockrill, Kilrush, Moyacomb, Newtownbarry, St Mary's, Tombrack
COOLGREANY	Ballylarkin, Ballynestragh, Coolgreany, Gorey Rural, Kilgorman, Kilnahue, Limerick, Monaseed, Wingfield	OLD ROSS	Ballyanne, Barrack Village, Barronstown, Carrigbyrne, Clonlea, Clonroche, Old Ross, Templeudigan, Whitemoor
ENNISCORTHY	Enniscorthy Rural, Enniscorthy Urban	ROSSLARE	Drinagh, Killinick, Kilscoran, Lady's Island, Rosslare, St Helen's, Tacumshane, Tomhaggard
FERNS	Balloughter, Ballycanew, Ballycarney, Ballymore, Ferns, Huntingtown, Kilboro, Kilcomb, Rossminogue, The Harrow, Tinnacross	TAGHMON	Adamstown, Carrick, Forth, Glynn, Kilbride, Kilgarvan, Taghmon, Wexford Rural, Whitechurch
FETHARD	Ballyhack, Fethard, Kilmokea, Rathroe and Templetown		
GOREY	Ardamine, Ballygarrett, Cahore, Courtown, Gorey Urban, Killenagh	TINTERN	Carnagh, Dunmain, Inch, Killesk, Oldcourt, Rochestown, Tintern, Whitechurch
KILLURIN	Artramont, Ballyhogue, Bree, Edermine, Killurin, Kilpatrick, The Leap	WEXFORD	Wexford No 1 Urban, Wexford No 2 Urban, Wexford No 3 Urban
KILTEALY	Ballindaggin, Castleboro, Killann, Killoughrim, Kiltealy, Marshalstown, Rossard		

First County Council 1899-1902

The first council elections were held on Thursday 6 April 1899 and the first meeting of the council took place on 22 April 1899.

ELECTED MEMBERS

Bolger, Bryan, Milltown, Ferns (died 1900)
Browne, Michael, Bridgetown
Cummins, John, Shielbaggin, Ramsgrange
Dempsey, Daniel, Killelan, Screen
Donohue, James, JP, Templeshannon, Enniscorthy
Doyle, James A, Templesheelin, Adamstown
Esmonde, Sir Thomas H Grattan, Bart, MP, Ballynestragh, Gorey
Hearn, James B, Chilcombe, New Ross
Hore, Edmond, Coldblow, Broadway
Mayler, James E, Harristown, Ballymitty
Murphy, Laurence, Ballykerogue, Campile
O'Connor, Patrick, JP, Ballycrystal, Newtownbarry (Bunclody)
Peacocke, Charles H, Belmont, Wexford
Power, Daniel, Ballinahask, Kilmuckridge
Ryan, Patrick, Westgate, Wexford
Sinnott, James, Bolinrush, Ferns
Smyth, Myles, Glascarrig, Ballygarrett
Walsh, John F, Crescent Quay, Wexford
Whitty, William (Junior), Pouldarrig, Oylegate

NOMINATED BY FORMER GRAND JURY

Doyne, Charles M, DL, Wells, Gorey
Stopford, Lord Viscount, Marlfield, Gorey
Walker, Capt. Thomas J, DL, Tykillen, Kyle, Wexford

EX OFFICIO MEMBERS

Codd, James, JP, Mayglass
Doyle, Owen, Galbally (died 27 January 1901)
Hickey, Michael, Garryrichard, Foulkesmills, New Ross
Redmond, M J, JP, Millmount, Gorey

ADDITIONAL MEMBERS

Bryan, Capt. Loftus A, Borrmount Manor, Enniscorthy
Fitzgerald, Lord Maurice, Johnstown Castle, Wexford (died 1901)

REPLACEMENTS

Bolger, John, Ferns (27 September 1900) in place of Bryan Bolger
Bolger, Thaddeus, Milltown, Ferns (8 March 1901) in place of Owen Doyle
Barrett-Hamilton, Captain Samuel, Kilmannock House, New Ross (13 June 1901) in place of Lord Maurice Fitzgerald

County Council 1902-1905

Date of election: 4 June 1902
Annual meeting: 16 June 1902

ELECTED MEMBERS

Ahearne, James, Cloonagh, Gusserane
Bolger, John, The Hotel, Ferns
Browne, Michael, Bridgetown
Cummins, John, JP, Ballyhack
Dempsey, Daniel, Killelan, Screen
Donohue, James, JP, Enniscorthy
Doyle, James A, Templesheelin, Adamstown
Esmonde, Sir Thomas H Grattan, Bart, Ballynestragh, Gorey
Furlong, Michael John, Templescoby, Enniscorthy
Hearn, James B, Chilcombe, New Ross
Hore, Edmond, Coldblow, Broadway
Kavanagh, Denis, Killincooleybeg, Kilmuckridge
King, Robert, Askinvillar, Kiltealy
Kinsella, Alexander, Gorey
Mayler, James E, Harristown, Ballymitty
Peacocke, C H, Belmont, Wexford
Ryan, Patrick, Westgate, Wexford (died 1903)
Sinnott, James, Bolinrush, Ferns
Walsh, John F, Spawell Road, Wexford

EX OFFICIO MEMBERS

Bolger, Thaddeus, JP, Milltown, Ferns
Codd, James, JP, Mayglass (Nominee, Wexford Rural District Council)
Doyle, Joseph D (Vice-Chairman, Gorey Rural District Council)
Hickey, Michael, Garryrichard, Foulkesmills

ADDITIONAL MEMBERS

Ennis, Mr M A, JP, Ardruadh, Wexford
Stopford, Lord Viscount, Marlfield, Gorey

REPLACEMENTS

Kehoe, John J, Main Street, Wexford (5 May 1903) in place of Patrick Ryan
Murphy, Michael, Ballygullick (June 1903) in place of James Codd
Sinnott, John, Ballybeg, Screen (13 June 1904) in place of Joseph D Doyle

County Council 1905-1908

Date of election: 30 May 1905
Annual meeting: 10 June 1905

ELECTED MEMBERS

Asple, Thomas, Galbally, Bree
Bolger, John, Ferns
Browne, Michael, Bridgetown
Cleary, Patrick, Whitechurch, Tintern (died 1907)
Codd, Marks, Woodlands, Kiltealy
Cummins, John, JP, Ballyhack
Dempsey, Daniel, Killelan, Screen
Donohue, James, JP, Enniscorthy
Doyle, James A, Templesheelin, Adamstown
Doyle, Matthew, Charlotte Street, Wexford
Esmonde, Sir Thomas H Grattan, Bart, Ballynestragh, Gorey
Hearn, James B, Chilcombe, New Ross
Hore, Edmond, Coldblow, Broadway
Kavanagh, Denis, Killincooleybeg, Kilmuckridge
Kehoe, John J, Main Street, Wexford
Kinsella, Alexander, Ballyloughan, Gorey
Mayler, James E, Harristown, Ballymitty
Peacocke, C H, Belmont, Wexford
Sinnott, James, JP, Bolinrush, Ferns

EX OFFICIO MEMBERS

Bolger, Thaddeus, JP, Milltown, Ferns
Hickey, Michael, Garryrichard, Foulkesmills, New Ross
Murphy, N C, JP, Coddstown, Tacumshane
Sinnott, John, Ballybeg, Screen

ADDITIONAL MEMBERS

Codd, James, Mayglass
Ennis, M A, JP, Ardruadh, Wexford

REPLACEMENTS

Forrestal, Walter, Ballykelly, New Ross (24 October 1907) in place of Patrick Cleary

County Council 1908-1911

Date of election: 1 June 1908
Annual meeting: 13 June 1908

ELECTED MEMBERS

Asple, Thomas, Galbally
Bolger, John, Ferns
Browne, Michael, Bridgetown
Codd, Marks, Woodlands, Kiltealy
Cummins, John, Ballyhack
Doyle, James A, Templesheelin, Adamstown
Doyle, Michael, Newtownbarry (Bunclody)
Esmonde, Sir T H G, Bart, MP, Ballynestragh, Gorey
Forrestal, Walter, Ballykelly, New Ross
Fortune, Patrick, Screen
Hearne, John S, JP, Bawnjames, New Ross (Chairman, New Ross Rural District Council)
Hore, Edmond, Coldblow, Rosslare (retired at end of this term)
Kavanagh, Denis, Killincooley, Monamolin (resigned 1 December 1909)
Kehoe, John J, South Main Street, Wexford
Kinsella, Alexander, JP, Gorey
Mayler, James E, Harristown, Ballymitty
O'Neill, Patrick, Enniscorthy
Peacocke, C H, Belmont, Wexford
Stafford, James Joseph, Main Street, Wexford

EX OFFICIO MEMBERS

Bolger, Thaddeus, Milltown, Ferns (died 2 June 1911)
Fanning, Patrick John, Aughullen, Kilanerin (Nominee, Gorey Rural District Council)
Hickey, Michael, Garryrichard, Foulkesmills, New Ross
Walsh, Gregory, Coolcull, Taghmon

ADDITIONAL MEMBERS

Codd, James, Mayglass
Ennis, M A, JP, Ardruadh, Wexford

REPLACEMENTS

Creane, Philip J, Coolroe, Kilmuckridge (9 September 1910) in place of Denis Kavanagh

County Council 1911-1914

Date of election: 31 May 1911
Annual meeting: 12 June 1911

ELECTED MEMBERS

Asple, Thomas, Galbally
Bolger, John, Ferns
Browne, Michael, Bridgetown (resigned 8 May 1912)
Cloney, Michael, Dungulph Castle, Fethard
Codd, Marks, Woodlands, Kiltealy
Doyle, James A, Templesheelin, Adamstown
Doyle, Michael (Junior), Cottage, Tagoat
Doyle, Michael (Senior), Newtownbarry (Bunclody)
Esmonde, Sir T H G, Bart, MP, Ballynestragh, Gorey (returned unopposed)
Esmonde, T L, Ballycoursey, Enniscorthy (died 10 October 1918 in the sinking of the *Leinster*)
Hearne, John S, Bawnjames, New Ross
Kinsella, Alexander, JP, Main Street, Gorey
Mayler, John T, Harristown, Ballymitty
O'Connor, John, Allen Street, Wexford (died March 1914)
O'Neill, Patrick, Enniscorthy
Peacocke, C H, JP, Belmont, Wexford
Rice, Richard A, Ballygarvan, Tintern
Sinnott, David, Ballylarkin, Kilmuckridge
Stafford, James J, South Main Street, Wexford

EX OFFICIO MEMBERS

Fanning, P J, Aughullen, Kilanerin
Hickey, Michael, Garryrichard, Foulkesmills, New Ross
Lynch, James, Templescoby, Enniscorthy
Rossiter, Patrick, Brookfield, Murrintown

ADDITIONAL MEMBERS

Codd, James, Mayglass
Stopford, Lord Viscount, Marlfield, Gorey

REPLACEMENTS

Gough, Michael, Ballyharty (12 June 1912) in place of Michael Browne
The council decided not to elect a member in place of John O'Connor 'owing to the near approach of the triennial elections'.

County Council 1914-1920

Date of election: 4 June 1914
Annual meeting: 16 June 1914

ELECTED MEMBERS

Asple, Thomas, Galbally, Bree
Barry, Louis, Poulrane, Bridgetown
Bolger, John, Ferns
Cloney, Michael, Dungulph, Fethard
Codd, Marks, Woodlands, Kiltealy
Doyle, James A, Templesheelin, Adamstown
Doyle, Michael, Tagoat
Esmonde, Sir T H G, Bart, MP, Ballynestragh, Gorey (returned unopposed)
Hearn, J S, JP, Bawnjames, New Ross (died 10 October 1918 in the sinking of the *Leinster*)
Keating, Philip, South Main Street, Wexford (died 1919)
Kehoe, John J, North Main Street, Wexford
Kinsella, Alexander, Main Street, Gorey
Mayler John T, Harristown, Ballymitty (died 1918)
O'Neill, Patrick, JP, Enniscorthy
Peacocke, C H, JP, Belmont, Wexford (died 1917)
Redmond, Joseph, Tinraheen, The Ballagh
Rice, R A, Ballygarvan, Tintern (resigned Oct/Nov 1915)
Scallan, Richard, Ballyvaloo, Curracloe
Whelan, Patrick, Bolinahaney, Newtownbarry (Bunclody)

EX OFFICIO MEMBERS

Cowman, Nicholas J, Monmore, Crossabeg
Hickey, Michael, Garryrichard, Foulkesmills, New Ross
Lynch, James, JP, Templescoby, Enniscorthy
Stopford, Lord Viscount, Marlfield, Gorey

ADDITIONAL MEMBERS

Codd, James, Mayglass
Stafford, J J, South Main Street, Wexford

REPLACEMENTS

Maddock, Michael, Ballyvalloge, Glynn (16 June 1917) in place of Charles H Peacocke
O'Byrne, John J, Cushenstown, Ballinaboola (12 November 1915) in place of R A Rice
Quigley, Patrick, JP, Faree, Foulkesmills (8 May 1918) in place of J T Mayler
O'Gorman, Peter N, JP, New Ross (3 December 1918) in place of J S Hearn
McGuire, W H, Mayor of Wexford (8 April 1919) in place of Philip Keating
Thorpe, William (June 1917) in place of Michael Hickey
Fowler, N J (June 1918) in place of Lord Stopford

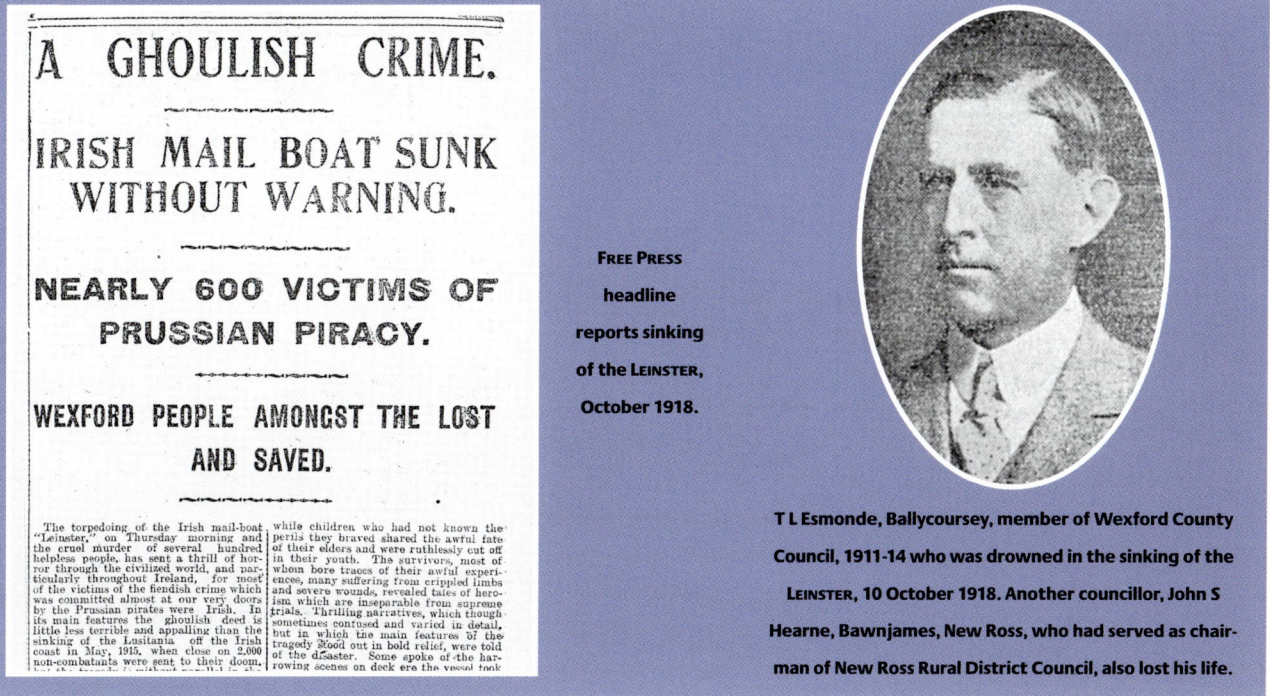

FREE PRESS headline reports sinking of the LEINSTER, October 1918.

T L Esmonde, Ballycoursey, member of Wexford County Council, 1911-14 who was drowned in the sinking of the LEINSTER, 10 October 1918. Another councillor, John S Hearne, Bawnjames, New Ross, who had served as chairman of New Ross Rural District Council, also lost his life.

PROPORTIONAL REPRESENTATION

Local elections took place, as normal, in 1914 and were due again in 1917. However, because of the 1914-18 war and the disturbed political situation in Ireland, they were postponed, first for a year, later to 1919 and eventually to 1920. In the meantime an election, run on the proportional representation system, had taken place in Sligo Corporation and it was decided that the same method would be used generally for the 1920 local elections. The form of proportional representation chosen was the single transferable vote in multi-seat constituencies. Previously, County Wexford comprised 124 district electoral divisions grouped into eighteen county electoral divisions. Each division returned one or two members to the relevant council, rural district or county. New electoral units became necessary in order to implement the proportional representation system.

The decision was to designate four county electoral areas returning a total of nineteen members to the county council. The inclusion of four ex officio members from the rural district councils and two additional co-opted members brought the strength to twenty-five. The membership of the rural district councils was substantially reduced. District electoral divisions, most of which had previously returned two members, were grouped into district electoral areas.

The New Organisation

County Council

Wexford electoral area	5 seats
Enniscorthy electoral area	4 seats
New Ross electoral area	5 seats
Gorey electoral area	5 seats
Ex officio members	4
Additional members	2

Rural District Councils

Wexford Rural District Council (formerly 69 members)

Ardcavan	3
Bannow	4
Bridgetown	5
Rosslare	5
Taghmon	3
Wexford Rural	4
TOTAL	24

Enniscorthy Rural District Council (formerly 71 members)

Ballyhuskard	6
Newtownbarry	5
Killann	4
Clonroche	5
Enniscorthy Rural	5
Ferns	3
TOTAL	28

Gorey Rural District Council (formerly 54 members)

Coolgreany	5
Gorey Town	4
Gorey Rural	6
Kilcomb	6
Monamolin	6
TOTAL	27

New Ross Rural District Council (formerly 54 members)

Old Ross	6
New Ross Rural	4
Carrigbyrne	6
Fethard	9
TOTAL	25

As can be seen, the urban areas of Wexford, Enniscorthy and New Ross, each of which had its own council, did not return members to either the county or rural district councils. They did, however, return members to the boards of guardians, which continued to administer the Poor Law and Medical Charities legislation. Only in New Ross was an election needed in these cases as the guardians for Wexford and Enniscorthy towns were returned unopposed. After the local elections, the boards of guardians comprised the members of the rural district councils with the directly elected guardians numbering thirteen in Wexford, six in Enniscorthy and eight in New Ross.

The 1920 elections were preceded, as usual, by

public meetings and advertisements aimed at making the candidates and their policies known to the voters. There was very little, however, about proportional representation itself and reaction to it was low-key. On the eve of the election the *Free Press* commented on the lack of public interest and speculated that this could be partly due to the inadequacy or absence of public information on the working of the system.

This was probably true because, apart from a request by the New Ross Urban District Council that the county council undertake an explanatory programme, there was virtually no discussion of the system at any of the council meetings. Nevertheless, the press did encourage the electorate to use the franchise. Polling was low and it is hard not to suppose that many people stayed away because of the perceived complexity of the new system.

Proportional representation is now the system of repeated choice in this country although it sometimes gives unexpected results. Between county and rural district councils and boards of guardians, the elections on 1 June 1920 involved twenty-two separate proportional representation counts in thirty electoral areas (candidates in eight areas were returned unopposed). Two of the counts deserve comment.

Wexford Electoral Area: Election 1 June 1920
Electorate: 11,600; vacancies: 5; candidates: 10; valid poll: 4,472; spoiled votes: 318; quota: 746

The results of the first count and the final outcome were:

Richard Corish	1351	Elected – 1st count
James Ryan	1145	Elected – 1st count
Christopher Culleton	680	Elected – 2nd count
Louis Barry	394	
Michael Doyle	271	Elected – later count
William R Devereux	199	
Greg Kelly	111	
James Walsh	142	
Michael Maddock	106	
John Sinnott	73	Elected – later count

On the transfer of Corish's surplus (605), C Culleton was elected with a surplus of 374. The transfer of this surplus and that of Dr James Ryan did not result in the election of any other candidate. They did, however, help to lift John Sinnott from the bottom of the poll to enable him to take a seat over the heads of the four Nationalist candidates, all of whom had polled between 45% and 50% higher than he had. On the final count he had one vote more than the unfortunate Louis Barry who had been a member of the council since the 1914 elections.

Killann Electoral Area: Election 1 June 1920
Four seats; valid poll: 984; quota: 197

Elected: James O'Leary, James Clince, E O'Connor, Thomas Doyle

The election in this area was unusual in that all four vacancies were filled on the first count when each of the successful candidates surpassed the quota. The 1920 elections, the first under proportional representation for rural district councils and boards of guardians, were also, ironically, the last because both bodies had been abolished by the time of the next local elections in 1925.

In 1925, the local elections, which fell on 23 June, were well heralded by *The People* editorials for several weeks in advance. The council strength was increased by two to twenty-seven, all to be elected directly because there were no longer rural district councils to supply ex officio members and the power of co-opting additional members had been repealed. The strength of the council remained at twenty-seven until 1942 when it was reduced to twenty-one, six from the Wexford electoral area and five each from Enniscorthy, New Ross and Gorey. The elections of 1942 coincided with the introduction of the county management system.

The membership of the council remains at twenty-one although changes to be implemented for the local elections in 1999 will see seven members elected from the Wexford electoral area, five each from Enniscorthy and New Ross and four from Gorey electoral area. These variations derive from demographic changes and are accommodated by alterations in the boundaries of the electoral areas which see seven district electoral divisions transferred from the Gorey to the Enniscorthy electoral area and five divisions moved from the Enniscorthy to the Wexford electoral area.

County Council 1920-1925

Date of election: 1 June 1920
Annual meeting: 18 June 1920

Local elections were due in 1917 but were postponed, first for a year, later to 1919 and eventually to 1 June 1920. This was the first election to the council under the proportional representation system. More changes of membership than would normally be expected took place during the lifetime of this council which coincided with the period of the War of Independence and the Civil War. The minutes of the council meetings record the resignations of several members for what appear to be rather vague reasons. The real causes were usually imprisonment or internment. However, this was only revealed later when members were welcomed home without any reticence as to their whereabouts while absent.

Mr J R Etchingham was elected chairman at the first meeting of this council. He was absent from the meeting, however, and did not officiate. On 29 June 1920 he became Minister for Fisheries in the first Dáil Éireann. The whole year was to pass without his attendance at a single council meeting and it was not until 30 August 1921 that he eventually took up the position to which he had been elected. In the meantime, another annual meeting had come around and Mr John J O'Byrne had been elected chairman 'until Mr J R Etchingham would be available'.

Dr James Ryan was elected vice-chairman at the meeting on 18 June 1920. Perhaps the newly elected members were conscious of the possibility of disruption during their tenure of office because they took the unusual step of electing a deputy vice-chairman, Mr Albert F Smith. In Etchingham's absence, Dr Ryan presided over most of the council meetings up to 7 December 1920. However, at their meeting on 22 December 1920 the council protested against the arrest and detention of Dr Ryan, John O'Byrne, A F Smith, John Sinnott and James Doyle, all members. Mr John Sinnott's letter of resignation, which came before the council on 7 December 1920, recited that he was 'anxious to resign his seat on the County Council for the six months of his imprisonment'.

ELECTED MEMBERS

Byrne, James, Boley, Ballycullane
Cloney, Michael, Dungulph, Fethard
Corish, Richard, William Street, Wexford
Culleton, Christopher, Ringaheen, Ballycogley
Cummins, John, Shielbaggin
Doyle, Michael, Tagoat
Etchingham, John R, TD, Ballinatray Lr, Courtown (died April 1923)
Hall, James, Tobergal, Boolavogue
Hughes, Matthew, Bunclody
Kavanagh, David, Ballylucas, Screen
Kehoe, Simon, Ballintubrid, Blackwater (died 10 January 1922)
Murphy, John, Main Street, Enniscorthy
O'Byrne, John J, Cushenstown, New Ross
O'Byrne, John, South Parade, Gorey (replaced)
Redmond, Michael, Misterin, Adamstown
Ryan, Dr James, Selskar Street, Wexford (replaced)
Shannon, James, Rathnure
Sinnott, John, Grattan Terrace, Wexford (resigned and replaced)
Smith, Albert F, Tomnalosset, Enniscorthy (replaced)

EX OFFICIO MEMBERS

Byrne, Michael, Ballinabearna, Ballywilliam
Doyle, James, Hillview Terrace, Enniscorthy
Kehoe, Owen, Coolgreany, Inch (resigned 4 January 1921)
Devereux, Gregory, Ballyfinogue, Killinick

ADDITIONAL MEMBERS

Lennon, Philip, New Ross (replaced)
Pender, John, Ferns

REPLACEMENTS

As a result of changes in the chairmanship of the rural district councils.
Furlong, W J, Dranagh, Caim (18 June 1921) in place of James Doyle
Doyle, Seamus (James) (26 June 1922) in place of W J Furlong
Hayes, Patrick, Kilmannon, Bridgetown (7 August 1923) in place of Gregory Devereux
Lawlor, James, Coolree, Ballindaggin (7 August 1923) in place of Seamus Doyle

OTHER REPLACEMENTS

O'Byrne, Patrick, Camolin (4 January 1921) in place of Owen Kehoe who resigned on moving to County Wicklow

Frith, Joseph, The Avenue, Gorey (7 August 1923) in place of J R Etchingham

O'Donoghue, Myles M, Raheenlusk, Kilmuckridge (13 March 1922) in place of Simon Kehoe

At the meeting on 4 January 1921, replacements were co-opted for six members who resigned because of imprisonment.

James Doyle was replaced by Thomas McCarthy, 17 George St, Enniscorthy

Philip Lennon was replaced by Mr Thomas Murphy, Skarke, New Ross

John O'Byrne (Gorey) was replaced by John J O'Byrne, Raheen, Camolin

Dr J Ryan was replaced by Edward P Foley, Main Street, Wexford

John Sinnott was replaced by Laurence Radford, Old Pound, Wexford

A F Smith was replaced by Patrick Buckley, Clonroche

However, even the co-optees were not safe. On 11 January 1921, the Enniscorthy Rural District Council was asked to nominate a member in place of Thomas McCarthy and the Wexford Trades and Labour Council was asked to name a substitute for Laurence Radford. Both men were under arrest.

Mr Thomas Walsh, High Street, Wexford, replaced Laurence Radford

Mr Walter J Furlong, Dranagh, Caim, replaced Thomas McCarthy

Fortview, headquarters of the council from March 1923 until March 1931. The house got its name from its view of the Rosslare Fort. It was formerly the residence of William Daniel, father of Mrs Barbara Newton Lett who wrote a diary of 1798. In the mid-nineteenth century it was the town house of the Sandwiths, a family of Cromwellian origin, and in 1901 it was occupied by Tom Healy, brother of Tim Healy, MP for Wexford (1880-83) and first Governor-General of the Irish Free State.

County Council 1925-1928

The Wexford County Electoral Areas Order 1925 fixed the composition of the council at twenty-seven members: seven each from Wexford, Gorey and New Ross areas and six from the Enniscorthy area.

Date of election: 23 June 1925
Annual meeting: 6 July 1925

ELECTED MEMBERS

Boggan, William, Hayestown Great
Clince, James, Caim, Enniscorthy
Cloney, Michael, Dungulph, Saltmills
Colfer, Patrick, Clonmines, Wellingtonbridge
Connors, John, Kilthomas, Ferns
Cooney, Thomas, 5 Robert Street, New Ross
Corish, Richard, TD, St Ibar's Tce, Wexford
Culleton, Christopher, Ringaheen, Ballycogley (declared disqualified, 9 November 1925)
D'Arcy, Timothy F, Annagh, Gorey (declared disqualified, 9 November 1925)
Doyle, Michael, TD, Walsheslough
Gaul, James, Carrigeen Street, Wexford
Gibbon, C M, Sleedagh, Wexford
Hall, James, Tobergal, Boolavogue, Ferns
Hayes, Patrick, Kilmannon, Cleariestown
Jordan, Michael, Ballyhamilton, Ballycarney
Kavanagh, David, Ballylucas, Screen
McCarthy, Thomas, George's Street, Enniscorthy
Mernagh, Aidan, Ballinaslaney, Oylegate
Murphy, Nicholas J, Kilmokea, New Ross
O'Byrne, Patrick, Camolin
O'Byrne, John, The Avenue, Gorey
O'Donoghue, Myles Michael, Raheenlusk, Kilmuckridge
Quin, Col. Richard Percival Wemyss, Borleagh, Inch
Shannon, James, Rathnure Lr
Thorpe, William F, Knockroe, New Ross
Walsh, James E, South Street, New Ross
White, John, Maxboley, Ballymitty

REPLACEMENTS

Pender, John, Ferns (14 December 1925) in place of Timothy D'Arcy
Rossiter, Thomas, Dempsey's Tce, Wexford (14 December 1925) in place of Christopher Culleton.

Timothy D'Arcy had hired a traction engine to a roads' contractor of the county council at the beginning of the year. Use of the machine continued until at least some days after the election. The council's solicitor advised that Mr D'Arcy was 'concerned' in the contract. Christopher Culleton had resigned as a rural district councillor in March 1925 to take work on contract repairing labourers' cottages for the Board of Health. He continued to work for some days after the election but ceased before he signed his declaration of acceptance of office a few days later. On the solicitor's advice, the council declared Culleton and D'Arcy disqualified.

County Council 1928-1934

Date of election: 26 June 1928
Annual meeting: 10 July 1928

Elected members

Armstrong, James, Glasslacken, Bunclody
Brennan, John, Currawn, Ballywilliam
Clince, James, Caim, Enniscorthy
Colfer, Patrick, Clonmines, Wellingtonbridge
Cooney, Thomas, 5 Robert Street, New Ross
Corish, Richard, TD, St Ibar's Villas, Wexford
Culleton, John, The Raven, Curracloe, Wexford
Cummins, John, Ballyhack, Arthurstown
D'Arcy, Timothy F, Annagh Lr, Inch, Gorey
Doran, John, Moneyhore, Enniscorthy
Doyle, Michael, Cottage, Tagoat
Gaul, James, 7 Roche's Terrace, Wexford
Gibbon, Col. C M, Sleedagh, Wexford
Hall, James, Tobergal, Boolavogue, Ferns
Hayes, Patrick, Kilmannon, Cleariestown
Jordan, Michael, TD, Ballyhamilton, Ferns
Keegan, W P, Esmonde Street, Gorey
Mayler, Thomas J, Harristown, Ballymitty
McCarthy, Thomas, 11 Rafter Street, Enniscorthy
Murphy, John, Ballykerogue, Campile (resigned 29 May 1933)
O'Byrne, Sean, The Avenue, Gorey
O'Ryan, Ellen, Tomcoole, Taghmon
Quin, Col. R P Wemyss, Borleagh, Inch
Roche, M M, Ballyseskin, Kilmore
Shannon, James, Rathnure Lower, Enniscorthy (died October 1933)
Smith, Myles, Glasscarrig South, Clonevan, Ballygarrett
Walsh, James E, 55 South Street, New Ross

Replacements

Hickey, Michael, Misterin, Adamstown (12 June 1933) in place of John Murphy
Kelly, John P, Kilpierce, Enniscorthy (11 December 1933) in place of James Shannon

Pictured at the opening of Feis Carman in Wexford Park, 1952. L to R: Senator Margaret Pearse, sister of the executed brothers, Padraig and Willie, Ellen O'Ryan, member of Wexford County Council 1928-1954, Dr Honoria Aughney, County Medical Officer and T D Sinnott, County Manager.

Until the 1960s, women were a rarity in the ranks of the elected members or as senior officials in county councils. Ellen ('Nell') Ryan of Tomcoole, Taghmon, was first elected to the council in 1928 and was for many years the only female councillor. During her years in public life, she was chairman of the Board of Health and Public Assistance and served on the Library Committee and Vocational Education Committee.

Dr Honoria Aughney was appointed CMO in 1947. She became legendary for her vehement single-mindedness in pushing through public health and safety regulations, particularly those in relation to tuberculosis and brucellosis.

County Council 1934-1942

Elections were due to be held in 1931 but under the Local Elections and Meetings (Postponement) Act 1931 they were postponed to 'not later than 15 July, 1934'.

Date of election: 26 June 1934
Annual meeting: 10 July 1934

ELECTED MEMBERS

Allen, Denis, Raheenagurren, Gorey
Bowe, James J, Kiltealy
Colfer, Patrick, Clonmines, Wellingtonbridge
Connors, John, Kilthomas, Ferns (resigned 12 February 1939)
Corish, Richard, TD, St Ibar's Villas, Wexford
Culleton, Christopher, Ringaheen, Ballycogley (resigned 26 March 1940)
Cullimore, William, Talbot Street, Wexford (resigned 11 April 1938)
Cummins, John, Ballyhack (resigned December 1937)
Day, John, Gollough, Kilmore
Doyle, Michael, Cottage, Tagoat (died 7 September 1942)
Gibbon, Col. C M, Sleedagh, Murrintown, Wexford (died December 1937)
Keegan, William P, Esmonde Street, Gorey
Kelly, John P, Kilpierce, Enniscorthy
Kinsella, William, Crosstown, Castlebridge
Lawlor, James, Coolree, Ballindaggin
Mayler, Thomas J, Harristown, Ballymitty
McCarthy, Thomas, George's Street, Enniscorthy
Murphy, Philip, Ballykerogue, Campile
O'Byrne, Sean, Gorey Avenue, Gorey
O'Ryan, Ellen, Tomcoole, Taghmon
Quin, Col. R P Wemyss, Borleagh, Inch
Redmond, Michael, Misterin, Adamstown
Redmond, Thomas, South Street, New Ross
Ronan, Patrick, Ferns (submitted resignation December 1939 but was persuaded by colleagues to withdraw it January 1940)
Smith, Myles, Glascarrig
Sweetman, Malachy, Ballycourceymore, Enniscorthy
Walsh, James E, Priory Street, New Ross

REPLACEMENTS

Bolger, Moses, Coolnaleen, Camolin (3 April 1939) in place of John Connors
Kehoe, Martin, Corragh, Bunclody (11 May 1942) in place of Moses Bolger who died 1942
Murphy, Sean, Tilladavins, Tomhaggard (9 May 1938) in place of William Cullimore
O'Neill, Patrick, Shanoo, Bridgetown (14 October 1940) in place of Sean Murphy who resigned 9 September 1940
Doyle, Raymond, Ballyharty, Bridgetown (10 January 1938) in place of Col. Gibbon
Kennedy, James, Shielbaggin, Ramsgrange (10 January 1938) in place of John Cummins
Swards, Joseph F, St Elmo, Rosslare Harbour (8 April 1940) in place of Christopher Culleton

County Council 1942-1945

The composition of the council was changed in 1942 to twenty-one members; six from the Wexford electoral area and five each from the Enniscorthy, New Ross and Gorey areas. The electoral areas remained unchanged.

Date of election: 19 August 1942
Annual meeting: 2 September 1942

Elected members

Allen, Denis, Raheenagurren, Gorey
Bowe, James J, Kiltealy
Brennan, Edward, Springmount, Killann, Rathnure
Byrne, Patrick, Camolin
Byrne, Thomas, 12 Columba's Villas, Wexford
Colfer, Patrick, Clonmines, Wellingtonbridge (resigned 11 October 1944)
Corish, Richard, TD, St Ibar's Terrace, Wexford
Day, John, Gollough, Kilmore
Fortune, James, Galbally, Bree
Gaul, James, Carrigeen Street, Wexford
Hickey, Michael, Garryrichard, Foulkesmills, New Ross
Keegan, William P, Ramsfort Park, Gorey
Kehoe, Martin, Corragh, Bunclody
Kennedy, James, Shielbaggin, Ramsgrange
McCarthy, Thomas, Rafter Street, Enniscorthy
Moran, Robert, Paul Quay, Wexford
O'Leary, John, TD, Shannon Hill, Enniscorthy
O'Ryan, Ellen, Tomcoole, Taghmon
Quin, Col. R P Wemyss, Borleagh, Inch (attended first meeting on 9 November 1942)
Redmond, Michael, Misterin, Adamstown
Walsh, James E, Priory Street, New Ross

Replacements

Kiely, William, Newbawn, Foulksmills (13 November 1944) in place of Patrick Colfer

County Council 1945-1950

Date of election: 14 June 1945
Annual meeting: 28 June 1945

Elected members

Allen, Denis, Raheenagurren, Gorey
Bowe, James J, Kiltealy
Brennan, Edward, Springmount, Killane, Rathnure (resigned 11 November 1946)
Byrne, Patrick, Camolin
Byrne, Thomas, 12 Columba's Villas, Wexford
Colfer, Patrick, Clonmines, Wellingtonbridge
Corish, Richard, TD, St Ibar's Terrace, Wexford (died July 1945)
Doran, James, NT, Tinnacross, Monageer
Fortune, Michael J, Slade, Fethard
Gaul, James, Carrigeen Street, Wexford
Keating, John, TD, Ballybough, Ballycogley
Kehoe, Martin, Corragh, Bunclody
McCarthy, Thomas, Rafter Street, Enniscorthy (died 1947)
Moran, Robert, Paul Quay, Wexford
O'Byrne, John, Gorey Avenue, Gorey
O'Leary, John, TD, Shannon Hill, Enniscorthy
O'Ryan, Ellen, Tomcoole, Taghmon
Power, Michael J, Tintern, Saltmills
Redmond, Michael, Misterin, Adamstown
Redmond, Thomas, Kilconnib, Ferns (Enniscorthy electoral area)
Redmond, Thomas, Mary Street, New Ross (New Ross electoral area)

Replacements

Franey, Edward, Knockmore, Caim (9 December 1946) in place of Edward Brennan
Sinnott, James, Kevin Barry Street, Wexford (8 October 1945) in place of Richard Corish
Hayes, Thomas, Court Street, Enniscorthy (15 December 1947), in place of Thomas McCarthy

County Council 1950-1955

Date of election: 20 September 1950
Annual meeting: 4 October 1950

Elected members

Allen, Denis, Raheenagurren, Gorey
Bowe, James J, Kiltealy
Browne, Sean, Pearse Road, Enniscorthy
Byrne, Thomas, 12 Columba's Villas, Wexford
Colfer, Patrick, Clonmines, Wellingtonbridge
Cullimore, Frank, South Main St, Wexford
Dempsey, Peter, Ballyconnigar Lr, Blackwater
Frayne, Edward, Knockmore, Caim
Furlong, John Joseph, Littlegraigue, Duncormick
Galvin, James, Ballyboggan, Wexford
Gaul, James, Carrigeen Street, Wexford
Graham, Patrick, Croghan Upper, Coolgreaney
Kehoe, Martin, Corragh, Bunclody
Kennedy, James Joseph, Riverview, Arthurstown
Kinsella, Patrick, Rosevilla, Gorey
O'Leary, John, Shannon Hill, Enniscorthy
O'Loughlin, T, Stable, Clonevin, Ballygarrett
O'Ryan, Ellen, Tomcoole, Wexford
Power, Michael Joseph, Tintern, Saltmills
Redmond, Thomas, Mary Street, New Ross
Sinnott, James, Kevin Barry Street, Wexford

Replacements

None

County Council 1955-1960

Date of election: 28 June 1955
Annual meeting: 12 July 1955

Elected members

Allen, Denis, TD, Raheenagurren, Gorey
Bowe, James J, Kiltealy
Boyce, James Jr, Cushenstown, Ballynabola
Browne, Seán, Pearse Road, Enniscorthy
Byrne, Thomas, 12 Columba's Villas, Wexford
Cullimore, Frank, South Main Street, Wexford
Curtin, Eugene, 9 Wygram Place, Wexford
D'Arcy, Timothy F, Annagh Lr, Inch (died 21 April 1958)
Fardy, Thomas, Rosspile, Foulksmills
Furlong, John Joseph, Littlegraigue, Duncormick
Galvin, James, Ballyboggan, Wexford
Hayes, Thomas J, 6 Court Street, Enniscorthy
Howlin, Thomas, Crossfarnogue, Kilmore Quay
Kennedy, James Joseph, Riverview, Arthurstown
Kinsella, Laurence, Johnstown, Clonegal
Kinsella, Patrick, Gorey Hill, Gorey
Minihan, Andrew, Kylebeg, Mountgarrett, New Ross
O'Leary, John, TD, Shannon Hill, Enniscorthy (died June 1959)
O'Loughlin, Thaddeus J, Stable, Clonevin, Ballygarrett
Redmond, Thomas, Knocknaveigh, The Ballagh
Sinnott, James, 36 Kevin Barry Street, Wexford (resigned May 1957)

Replacements

Nolan, Evelyn, 1 Shannon Hill, Enniscorthy (10 August 1959) in place of John O'Leary
Doran, James, Rathaspick (8 July 1957) in place of James Sinnott
D'Arcy, Michael, Annagh Lr, Inch, Gorey (9 June 1958) in place of Timothy F D'Arcy

County Council 1960-1967

Date of election: 29 June 1960
Annual meeting: 13 July 1960

ELECTED MEMBERS

Bowe, James J, Kiltealy
Browne, Seán, TD, Pearse Road, Enniscorthy
Byrne, Thomas, 12 Columba's Villas, Wexford
Carthy, Leo, Airdownes Great, Kilrane
Corish, Nicholas P, Iverna, St John's Road, Wexford
Cullimore, Frank, 112 South Main Street, Wexford
Curtin, Eugene, County Hotel, Wexford
D'Arcy, Michael, Annagh Lr, Inch
Dunbar, Martin, Castleland, Ferns
Esmonde, William, Bachelor's Hall, Hayestown, Wexford
Fardy, Thomas, Rosspile, Foulksmills (resigned 13 April 1964)
Funge, Thomas, 17 Main Street, Gorey
Furlong, John Joseph, Littlegraigue, Duncormick
Hayes, Thomas J, 6 Court Street, Enniscorthy
Kennedy, James J, Riverview, Coleman, Arthurstown
Kinsella, Laurence, Johnstown, Clonegal
McDonald, Patrick, Duncannon
Minihan, Andrew, Mountgarrett, New Ross
Nolan, Evelyn, 1 Shannon Hill, Enniscorthy (resigned 14 August 1961)
O'Loughlin, Thaddeus J, Stable, Clonevin, Gorey
Redmond, Thomas, Knocknaveigh, The Ballagh

REPLACEMENTS

Delaney, Thomas, Courtnacuddy, Enniscorthy (11 September 1961) in place of Evelyn Nolan
Rothwell, Benjamin T A, Adamstown (8 June 1964) in place of Thomas Fardy

County Council 1967-1974

In the June 1967 local elections candidates were allowed, for the first time, to show their political party affiliation on the ballot papers.

Date of election: 28 June 1967
Annual meeting: 12 July 1967

ELECTED MEMBERS

Bowe, James J, Kiltealy, Fine Gael
Browne, Seán, Pearse Road, Enniscorthy, Fianna Fáil
Byrne, Thomas, 12 St Columba's Villas, Wexford, Labour Party
Carthy, Leo, Airdownes, Broadway, Non-Party
Corish, Desmond, 36 North Main Street, Wexford, Labour Party
Curtin, Eugene, Coolcotts, Wexford, Fianna Fáil (resigned 11 February 1974)
D'Arcy, Michael J, Annagh, Gorey, Fine Gael
Doyle, Andy, Island Road, Enniscorthy, Labour Party
Dunbar, Martin, Castlelands, Ferns, Labour Party (died 22 January 1972)
Dunne, Thomas, Knockmore, Caim, Fianna Fáil (died 12 March 1971)
Esmonde, Bill, Bachelor's Hall, Wexford, Fine Gael
Funge, Thomas, Main Street, Gorey, Fianna Fáil
Furlong, John J, Littlegraigue, Duncormick, Fianna Fáil (resigned 28 February 1970)
Hart, Michael, Tinnock, Campile, Fine Gael
Howlin, Thomas, Crossfarnogue, Kilmore Quay, Fianna Fáil
Kennedy, James J, Riverview, Arthurstown, Fianna Fáil (died 13 September 1968)
McDonald, Patrick, Duncannon, Labour Party
Murphy, Rory, Ballinavocran, Bunclody, Fianna Fáil
O'Brien, Laurence, Maudlins, New Ross, Fine Gael (resigned December 1970)
O'Loughlin, Thaddeus J, Stable, Ballygarrett, Fine Gael
Quirke, John, The Oil, Oylegate, Fine Gael

REPLACEMENTS

Curtis James, Loughnageer, Foulkesmills (11 May 1970) in place of John J Furlong
Dunbar, Rosaleen, Corner House, Ferns (13 March 1972) in place of Martin Dunbar

Kennedy, Martin, Shielbaggin, Ramsgrange (11 November 1968) in place of James J Kennedy

O'Gorman, Sean, River, Adamstown (December 1969) in place of Martin Kennedy who resigned in November 1969

Sinnott, Michael J, Garrywilliam House, Crossabeg (May 1971) in place of Thomas Dunne

Ronan, Patrick, 8 Mary Street, New Ross (11 January 1971) in place of Laurence O'Brien

Ryan, Martin, Old Boley House, Forth Commons, Wexford (11 March 1974) in place of Eugene Curtin

County Council 1974-1979

Date of election: 18 June 1974
Annual meeting: 2 July 1974

Elected members

Allen, Lorcan, Raheenagurren, Gorey, Fianna Fáil

Bolger, David F, Millmount, Gorey, Fine Gael (resigned 13 February 1978)

Bowe, James J, Kiltealy, Fine Gael

Browne, Seán, Pearse Road, Enniscorthy, Fianna Fáil (resigned 10 September 1977)

Byrne, Hugh, Air Hill, Fethard-on-Sea, New Ross, Fianna Fáil

Carthy, Leo, Airdownes, Broadway, Non-Party

Corish, Philip, Belvedere Road, Wexford, Labour Party

Curtis, James, Loughnageer, Foulksmills, Co. Wexford, Fianna Fáil

D'Arcy, Michael J, Annagh, Gorey, Fine Gael

Doran, Joseph, Ballinastraw, Monomolin, Gorey, Fianna Fáil

Doyle, Andy, Island Road, Enniscorthy, Labour Party

Doyle, Avril, Rocklands, Wexford, Fine Gael

Dunbar, Thomas, Corner House, Ferns, Labour Party

Hart, Michael, Tinnock, Campile, Fine Gael

Howlin, Thomas, Crossfarnogue, Kilmore Quay, Fianna Fáil

Mahony, James, 84 Bishopswater, Wexford, Non-Party

McDonald, Patrick, Duncannon, Labour Party

O'Gorman, Sean, River, Adamstown, Fianna Fáil

Quirke, John, The Oil, Oylegate, Fine Gael

Ryan, Martin Joseph, Old Boley House, Forth Commons, Wexford, Fianna Fáil

Sinnott, Michael Joseph, Garrywilliam House, Crossabeg, Wexford, Fianna Fáil

Replacements

Dunne, Rory, Ballinakill, Enniscorthy (10 October 1977) in place of Seán Browne

Bolger, Deirdre, Millmount, Gorey (13 March 1978) in place of David F Bolger

County Council 1979-1985

Date of election: 9 June 1979
Annual meeting: 21 June 1979

ELECTED MEMBERS

Allen, Lorcan, Raheenagurren, Gorey, Fianna Fáil
Bolger, Deirdre, Millmount, Gorey, Fine Gael
Browne, John A, Kilcannon, Enniscorthy, Fianna Fáil
Browne, John T, Millquarter, Newbawn, Fine Gael
Byrne, Gus, 19 Thomas Clarke Place, Wexford, Fianna Fáil
Byrne, Hugh, Air Hill, Fethard-on-Sea, New Ross, Fianna Fáil
Carthy, Leo, Lake View, Broadway, Non-Party
Codd, Patrick, Ballinahallen, Enniscorthy, Fine Gael
Corish, Brendan, Belvedere Road, Wexford, Labour Party
Curtis, James, Loughnageer, Foulksmills, Co. Wexford, Fianna Fáil
D'Arcy, Michael, Annagh, Inch, Gorey, Fine Gael (resigned February 1985)
Doyle, Avril, Rocklands, Wexford, Fine Gael
Dunne, Rory, Ballinakill, Enniscorthy, Fianna Fáil
Gahan, James, Ballycarrigan, Ferns, Fine Gael
Howlin, Thomas, Crossfarnogue, Kilmore Quay, Fianna Fáil
Murphy, Rory, Ballinavocran, Bunclody, Fianna Fáil
North, Denis, 6 Charleton Hill, New Ross, Labour Party
Quirke, John, The Oil, Oylegate, Fine Gael
Roche, John, 21 Corish Place, Wexford,
Sinnott, Michael Joseph, Garrywilliam House, Crossabeg, Wexford, Fianna Fáil
Walsh, Jim, Pondfields, New Ross, Fianna Fáil

REPLACEMENTS

D'Arcy, Francis, Mount St Benedict, Hollyfort, Gorey (11 March 1985) in place of Michael D'Arcy

County Council 1985-1991

Date of election: 20 June 1985
Annual meeting: 4 July 1985

ELECTED MEMBERS

Allen, Lorcan, Raheenagurren, Gorey, Fianna Fáil
Bolger, Deirdre, Millmount, Gorey, Fine Gael
Bolger, Jack, Marshalstown, Enniscorthy, Fine Gael
Browne, John A, Kilcannon, Enniscorthy, Fianna Fáil
Browne, John T, Millquarter, Old Ross, Fine Gael
Byrne, Gus, 19 Thomas Clarke Place, Wexford, Fianna Fáil
Byrne, Hugh, Air Hill, Fethard-on-Sea, New Ross, Fianna Fáil
Carthy, Leo, Lake View, Broadway, Non-Party
Curtis, Jimmy, Loughnageer, Foulksmills, Co. Wexford, Fianna Fáil
D'Arcy, Francis J, Mount St Benedict, Gorey, Fine Gael (resigned May 1987)
Doyle, Avril, Rocklands, Wexford, Fine Gael
Doyle, Seán, 2 Esmonde Road, Enniscorthy
Howlin, Brendan, 7 Upper William Street, Wexford, Labour Party
Howlin, Tommy, Crossfarnogue, Kilmore Quay, Fianna Fáil (died 1 January 1987)
Murphy, Joe, Knockskemolin, Wells, Gorey, Fianna Fáil
Murphy, Rory, Ballinavocran, Bunclody, Fianna Fáil
Reck, Padge, Mulgannon, Wexford, Non-Party
Roche, John, 21 Corish Place, Wexford
Sinnott, Michael J, Garrywilliam House, Crossabeg, Fianna Fáil
Walsh, Jim, Parkfield, New Ross, Fianna Fáil
Whelan, Seamus, Ballycullane, New Ross, Fianna Fáil
Yates, Ivan, Blackstoops, Enniscorthy, Fine Gael

REPLACEMENTS

Lambert, Robert, Ballyaddragh, Kilrane (2 February 1987) in place of Tommy Howlin
D'Arcy, Michael, Annagh, Gorey (8 June 1987) in place of Francis D'Arcy

County Council 1991-1999

Date of election: 27 June 1991
Annual meeting: 11 July 1991

Elected members

Allen, Lorcan, Raheenagurren, Gorey, Fianna Fáil
Bolger, Deirdre, Millmount, Gorey, Fine Gael
Bolger, John, Marshalstown, Enniscorthy, Fine Gael
Browne, John A, Kilcannon, Enniscorthy, Fianna Fáil (ceased February 1992)
Browne, John T, Millquarter, Old Ross, Fine Gael
Byrne, Gus, 19 Thomas Clarke Place, Wexford, Fianna Fáil
Byrne, Hugh, Air Hill, Fethard-on-Sea, New Ross, Fianna Fáil
Carthy, Leo, Lake View, Broadway, Non-Party
Corish, Helen, Woodhelven, 7 Parkview, Wexford
Curtis, James, Loughnageer, Foulksmills, Co. Wexford, Fianna Fáil
D'Arcy, Michael J, Annagh, Gorey, Fine Gael
Doyle, Avril, Rocklands, Wexford, Fine Gael (ceased 27 January 1995)
Doyle, Sean, 2 Esmonde Road, Enniscorthy
Gahan, James, Ballycarrigeen, Ferns, Co. Wexford, Fine Gael
Howlin, Brendan, 7 Upper William Street, Wexford, Labour Party (ceased 12 January 1993)
Murphy, Rory, Ballinavocran, Bunclody, Fianna Fáil
O'Brien, Laurence, Ballinamona, Campile, New Ross, Fine Gael
Reck, Padge, Mulgannon, Wexford, Non-Party
Sinnott, Michael J, Garrywilliam House, Crossabeg, Fianna Fáil (died 16 March 1995)
Walsh, Jim, Parkfield, New Ross, Fianna Fáil
Yates, Ivan, Blackstoops, Enniscorthy, Fine Gael (ceased 15 December 1994)
Members who 'ceased' did so automatically on appointment as ministers or ministers of state in the national government.

Replacements

Byrne, Peter, Borrmount, Enniscorthy (9 March 1992) in place of John A Browne
John A Browne (17 May 1996) in place of Peter Byrne who resigned 30 April 1996
Byrne, Vincent, 'Erin Cottage', St Peter's Square, Wexford (8 February 1993) in place of Brendan Howlin
Carr, Thomas, Corish Memorial Hall, Wexford (13 June 1994) in place of Vincent Byrne who resigned 31 May 1994
Walsh, John, Crosshue, Blackwater (13 February 1995) in place of Ivan Yates
Codd, Pat, Dungeer, Taghmon (13 February 1995) in place of Avril Doyle
Sinnott, Michelle, Garrywilliam House, Crossabeg (12 June 1995) in place of Michael J Sinnott
Kavanagh, Patrick, Drumgoold Lr, Enniscorthy (12 October 1998) in place of John Walsh who died 18 June 1998

COUNTY HALL, WEXFORD

The buildings now known as County Hall were built as the County Jail by the grand jury in 1807-1808 on a site acquired from one Thomas Jones. The architect and builder was a Mr Morrison and the contract price was reported to be £10,000. The distinctive castellated front entrance, described as 'two turnkeys' lodges', was added after 1840, as was the 'front' building which now contains the courtroom and other offices.

The property was used for its original purpose for just under one hundred years. No doubt it housed some serious criminals from time to time because there are contemporary reports of executions, but the majority were probably convicted of minor crimes. In 1901 the number detained stood at twenty-six males and twelve females, most of whom were serving sentences of one to three months for such offences as larceny, disorderly conduct and drunkenness. Two female prisoners were each accompanied by an infant. The governor, eight warders and two assistant matrons were also in residence in the complex.

It ceased to be used as a gaol in September 1904, by which time it incorporated (or had in the course of the years): a male prison (66 cells); a female prison (49 cells); a marshalsea or debtors' prison; a governor's residence; warders' quarters; a Protestant chapel; a Catholic chapel; an infirmary; workshops and laundry; and a treadmill. It also had its own water supply.

Ownership of the property transferred by law to the county council, as successors to the grand jury, a year after it ceased to be used as a gaol. The formal handing over was on 16 September 1905. At that time the council's headquarters and assembly room were in the Wexford Courthouse, a substantial building situated on the quay, just opposite the site of the present bridge. The council was not really prepared for its new acquisition which came with a recurring liability of £223 (equivalent to about £16,700 in 1998) to the successors of Thomas Jones. The councillors were probably happy, therefore, to enter an arrangement in 1908 to let the property to the Sisters of St John of God for use as a rehabilitation centre for 'inebriate women'. The complex was known as St Brigid's Home for Inebriate Women until 1920 when the sisters found that the service was no longer viable and, by mutual consent, returned the property to the council in August.

The council, which had declared allegiance to Dáil Éireann in June, quickly moved from the courthouse and held its first meeting in the former St Brigid's or Old Jail on 7 October, 1920. The first official use of the name 'County Hall' was recorded in the minutes of that meeting. It is by this name that it has been known ever since although the explanatory titles 'St Brigid's' and 'Old Jail' were frequently appended for several years afterwards.

The council's occupation did not last long. On 4 July 1921, the property was commandeered by the Royal Irish Constabulary for use as a barracks. It was vacated by them on 11 March 1922. In the meantime council meetings took place in the Wexford Workhouse and the Town Hall. The council took up residence again for its meeting on 3 April 1922, only to be disturbed once more by military requisition, this time by the Free State army which took possession from February 1923 until 30 October 1924. On 13 March 1923, three Republican prisoners, James Parle (Taghmon), Patrick Hogan (Wexford) and John Creane (Taghmon), were executed by firing squad in the yard behind the old gaol.

Under pressure for accommodation, the council purchased the substantial residence, Fortview (see p 111), on the opposite side of the Spawell Road, in March 1923 and retained it for the next eight years before moving back, once again, to the County Hall on 23 March 1931. The County Hall has remained the council's headquarters since then although the buildings have undergone many changes. Several of the buildings shown in early ordnance maps have been removed as have the walls which delineated the sixteen exercise yards that existed in 1837. All of the 'prison' buildings which remain have been modified to a greater or lesser degree. Many of the modifications were planned and executed by the council's engineering, architectural and construction staff. Major refurbishments took place in 1933, 1955, 1980, 1985, 1991, 1994 and 1995. In 1977 a new engineering services block was added. The building which retains the strongest resemblance to its original purpose today is the former women's prison where many of the forty-nine cells still exist.

APPENDIX II

Rural District Councils 1899

RURAL DISTRICT COUNCILS (RDCs) were established and elected at the same time as the county councils. They were distinct legal entities with corporate existence and directly elected membership. However, they also had characteristics of council committees; for example their decisions on contracts and finance were subject to review by the county council. The chairman of each RDC, or another member in his or her place, became an ex officio member of the county council.

The number of members in each RDC depended on the number of district electoral divisions within the rural district. There were usually two members per division but more where an urban area was included. Consequently, the membership of the rural councils was numerically large; for example, Enniscorthy RDC had sixty-three elected members. Each rural council was required to co-opt three additional members from amongst those who were previously entitled to be ex officio poor law guardians (usually justices of the peace). The councils had the further option of electing three additional members to their numbers.

The first meetings of the Wexford Rural District Councils were held on 15 April 1899.

Enniscorthy Rural District Council: Elected members

Michael Murphy	Daniel J O'Callaghan	Thomas A Rudd
Patrick Carty	James Murphy	Wm Kennedy
John Shea	Edward O'Connor	Michael Kennedy
Aidan Whelan	John Furlong	Daniel Doyle
Owen Doyle	Thomas Cleary	William Kennedy
Thomas Asple	Aidan Kelly	Patrick Canning
John J Couligan	Leonard Cardwell	Thomas Fitzpatrick
Mark Kavanagh	James Hennessey	Justin Sutton
Thaddeus Bolger JP	Thomas Whelan	Peter Kehoe
Denis Kavanagh	John Bolger	Martin Doyle
Andrew Brien	James Browne	Patrick Crane
Philip Redmond	Patrick Kehoe	John Walsh
John Cooney	Arthur Gough	Thomas Kavanagh
John Sinnott	Myles Cooney	James Lynch
Michael Cowman	Richard Forrestal	Daniel Nolan
Denis Lacy	John Forrestal	Thos Behan
Moses Dunne	Marks Codd	Michael O'Neill
Morgan Lacy	Myles Slevin	James Lambert
John Dillon	Philip Redmond	Moses Fortune

Moses Dempsey	John S Atkins	Thomas Carroll
Thomas Nolan	James Doyle	John Mernagh

James Doyle and John Mernagh were recorded as absent from the first meeting.

CO-OPTED FROM FORMER POOR LAW GUARDIANS

John Cullen JP, James O'Gorman JP, Thomas Prandy JP

ADDITIONAL MEMBERS

Michael Doyle, James Johnson, James Nolan

New Ross No 1 Rural District Council: Elected members

Denis Cummins	John Murphy	John Kelly
Patrick Doyle	Patrick R Barron	James Brennan
Hugh Murphy	Michael Byrne Jr	Patrick Tobias Rossiter
John Frayne	Thomas Mooney	Denis McGrath
John Power	Henry King	John Clooney
Martin J Kenny	Thomas Neville	Abraham J Stephens
Edward Neville	John Carty	Henry J Williams
Martin Harrington	John Cummins	Edward Evoy
Nicholas Howlett	William Keane	Nicholas Cooney
Michael Hickey	Joseph T Jeffares	Moses Murphy
Henry P Gahan	Patrick Bailey	Edward Loughlin Jr
Martin Furlong	Bryan O'Neill	Michael Conway
John Redmond	William Hornick	James Power
Charles Mullins	James Ryan	Michael Breen
Patrick Cleary	James Shannon	Robert Power
James Quinn	William Thorpe	

CO-OPTED FROM FORMER POOR LAW GUARDIANS

P J Roche JP, James Hutchinson JP, Captain Samuel Barrett-Hamilton JP

ADDITIONAL MEMBERS

The council decided not to exercise its option to elect three additional members.

Gorey Rural District Council: Elected members

Sir Thomas H G Esmonde MP	Viscount Stopford	John Sinnott
William Graham	Captain Loftus A Bryan	Luke Smith
M J Redmond JP	Captain A W M Richards	Thomas Middleton
James Whithers	James Kavanagh	Laurence Condron
Bernard Flusk	Edward Donohue	William Sheehan
Patrick Finn	John R Tomkins	John Smith
G J Stephens	James Maguire JP	John Cullen
Matthew Reddy	John Hall	Thomas Smith
John J Byrne	John Doyle	Philip Creane JP
Bartholomew O'Reilly	Edward Doyle	Edward Hill
Patrick Hughes	James Sheridan	Joseph D Doyle

John Kehoe	Valentine Crowe	David Sinnott
Peter Dempsey	John G Poole	Alexander Kinsella
Patrick Fanning	Patrick Sullivan	Thomas Mulligan
William Redmond	Thomas Nolan	Michael Lyons
Michael O'Connor	Daniel Kennedy	George Walsh
Thomas Scallan	Moses Walsh	Hugh Toole
	Morgan Condren	William A Ryan

Morgan Condren and William A Ryan were recorded as absent from the first meeting.

Co-opted from former poor law guardians
John McDonald JP, James Jones JP, James Sinnott JP

Additional members
Patrick Stafford, Thomas Pierce, J Redmond

Wexford Rural District Council: Elected members

Lord Maurice Fitzgerald	Charles H Peacocke JP	Martin French
Andrew Joyce	James Codd JP	James Furlong
Patrick Lambert	B H Roice JP	John Sinnott (Glenduff)
John Lambert	Michael Sinnott	John Sinnott (Keelogues)
Edmond Doyle	John Codd	Denis L O'Brien
Felix Adams	Laurence Donoghue	Thomas Kehoe
Bartholomew Furlong	Patrick Fortune	Hugh Connors
John Furlong	John Laffan	James Cullen
James Codd	Edward Redmond	James Daly
Patrick Rossiter	John Codd	John Murphy
Michael Doyle	Michael Cogley	John Ryan
Charles Etchingham	John Howlin	Simon Walsh
William Murphy	John E Richards	Richard Joyce
Luke Stafford	Thomas Devereux	John Walsh
Patrick Bourke	John Kane	Richard Murphy
John P Keating	Michael Browne	Patrick Rowe
Michael Murphy	Robert O'Connor	Michael Staples
William Richard Devereux	John Clancy	James Mayler
Nicholas Scallan	Patrick Scallan	Michael Sinnott
Denis Malone	Patrick Walsh	John Barry
John Byrne	Patrick Brien	

Co-opted from former poor law guardians
Patrick Codd, J J Roche, Major Boyse

Additional members
Lady Maurice Fitzgerald, William Pettit, Mrs M A Ennis

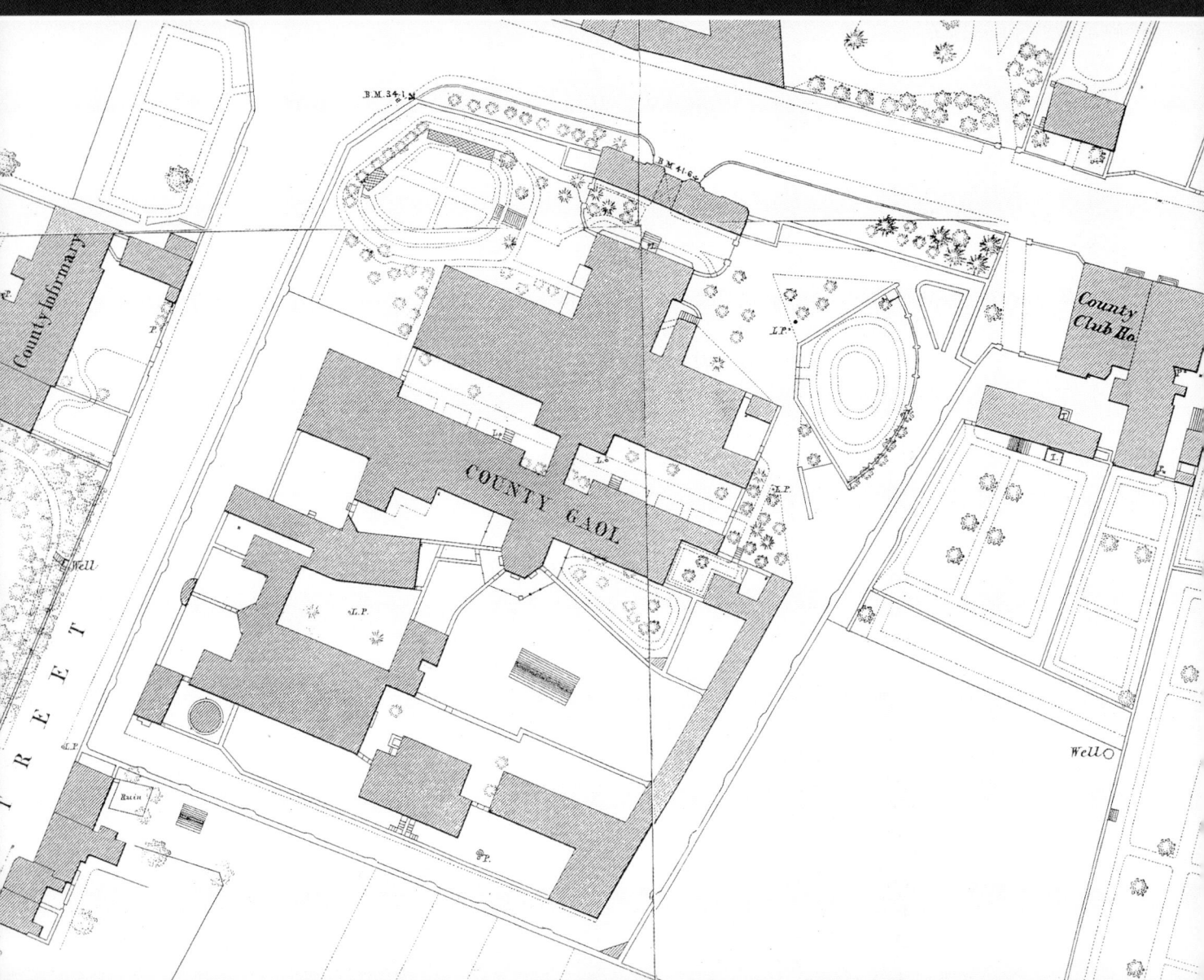

Plan of County Jail, 1883.

APPENDIX III

Chronology

Year	Date	Event
1898	12 August	Local Government (Ireland) Act enacted.
1899	16 January	The first elections under the Local Government (Ireland) Act 1898 held in boroughs, urban districts and municipal towns.
	31 March	By 31 March 1899 the boards of guardians had prepared schemes under the Labourers (Ireland) Act 1883 to provide 1,036 cottages of which between 850 and 900 had been built. In 1899 these houses passed to the rural district councils which, as rural sanitary authorities, became responsible for implementing the Act from then forward.
	6 April	The first elections under the Local Government (Ireland) Act 1898 for county and rural district councillors (and poor law guardians in urban districts).
	10 April	At their meeting in April 1899 Wexford Corporation briefly discussed the use of a steamroller but rejected the idea because of fears that the heavy machine would break through their sewers. They decided instead to suggest that the county council should initiate the practice.
	15 April	First annual meetings of Wexford, Enniscorthy, New Ross and Gorey Rural District Councils.
	22 April	First meeting of Wexford County Council held in grand jury room, Courthouse, Wexford.

Elevation of Wexford Courthouse facade from 1863 reconstruction plans.

27 May The issue of steamrolling was raised by the county surveyor at the meeting of the Wexford Rural District Council on 27 May, when he inquired if they had any idea about using steam-rollers. In reply to questions he said he thought it would cost £1,000 to buy a machine and that the best plan would be to hire a machine to do the work by contract. 'Steam-rollers would be of no use at all for ordinary maintenance contracts. The cost in Dublin County to do the metalling, not in a very first-class way as it was done in England, but to put on a coat of stones and roll them over, was at least £1 per perch.'

Mr Peacocke said he would be in favour of having a steam-roller procured if it could be found that the cost would, even ultimately, be the same as under the present system.

Mr Webster – 'With the steamroller it is utterly impossible to do it at the same price. It is utterly out of the question.'

The matter was left in abeyance.

1899 15 June When their first invitation for tenders appeared in June 1899 the Wexford Rural District Council advertised for twenty-nine contracts for maintaining roads in good condition and repair 'at a price not exceeding that specified in each case' for a period of four and a half years. The odd term was with a view to having future contracts expire in the month of March.

The following are typical of the contracts on offer:

> 312 perches from Rochestown Cross-roads, through Ballingale to the bounds of Bargy, not to exceed 5d per perch per annum
>
> 620 perches between Ballyhealy Bank and Ballask Cross-roads, not to exceed 6d per perch per annum
>
> 866 perches between the Mill of Rags to Cullenstown Gate by Ballytore Cross, not to exceed 6d per perch per annum
>
> 489 perches leading from Kilmore Chapel Gate to the Pier of Kilmore, not to exceed 1s per perch per annum (half the amount from County at Large)
>
> 917 perches between the abutment of the new free bridge of Wexford and the bridge at Castlebridge, not to exceed 4s per perch per annum.

29 June Under the 1898 Act the county surveyor was required to report to the various councils on the condition of the public works in their areas. This duty fell to Mr Henry Webster, who had previously served with the grand jury and who had transferred as county surveyor to the county council on its establishment. In his first report he said:

> The roads and public Works in the County are being fairly well maintained, but there are some exceptions

and I have to refuse to certify for some contracts.

I have to bring to your notice in particular contract No 37 Gorey which was in a very bad condition and I would ask you to authorise me to prosecute the Contractor if, on my next inspection, I don't find a marked improvement.

The work at Kilmore Pier is progressing well, but I fear I shall require about £85 more to complete the repairs at the back of the pier, and also to make good the damage done by the *SS Gloucester* to the wharf wall.

In accordance with the wishes of the Wexford Rural District Council I am preparing a report to be forwarded to the Treasury pointing out the desirability of extending the breakwater at Kilmore in order to prevent the harbour from silting up, the idea being that the Government might be induced to give a grant to this necessary work.

With reference to the schedule of Main Roads I wish to mention that under the Local Government Act, I believe that you cannot include the streets of Wexford Urban District in the declaration of Main Roads. I would therefore ask you to exclude these Streets from your final declaration.

In accordance with your directions I have measured the roads from Gorey to Wicklow Gap &c., with a view to have same included in the schedule of Main Roads. With this addition the Main Roads of Gorey District would be the same proportion (viz. one sixth) to the mileage of the District as in the other Rural Districts.

I beg to point out the difficulty there is in many parts of the County to obtain suitable material and that under the new Act you are empowered to purchase quarries and machinery. I hope you will see your way to acquire a few good quarries in central positions and perhaps later on you will be able to experiment with road machinery. At first I would recommend hiring of machinery in preference to purchase of same.

It would be well if you would make some arrangement as to the serving of ten days notice on faulty contractors. I would suggest that you would authorise me to serve these notices and so save delay. Also, in case I have to take over any road for any quarter year the men I would employ to put on the road in repair should be paid on fortnightly pay sheets from a small Subsidiary Account which account would afterwards be refunded with the Contractor's salary. If this plan be adopted I know from experience that the effect on the roads will be better than a prosecution and will not cause any increase in expenditure for the road.

The following contracts have expired or will expire on or before 30th September 1899 and I would recommend that the contracts be renewed from that date for a term of 4½ years, unless where otherwise stated, and that the cost for same be levied off the County at Large.

(1) To keep in repair for 4½ years the footpaths roadway &c., over the New Free Bridge of Wexford including painting and to care the opening machinery. Not to exceed £100 per annum.

(2) To keep in repair for 4½ years the roadway &c., over Edermine Bridge and to care the opening machinery. Not to exceed £8 per annum.

(3) To care for 5 years the opening machinery of Mountgarrett bridge and to open same when required. Not to exceed £9 per annum.

(4) To keep in repair for 4½ years from the 1st September 1899 the Bridge of the Deeps with the roadway over same and the wooden railing adjoining East side of said bridge. Not to exceed £45 per annum.

	October	Loan of £6,440 raised from Commissioners of Public Works by Enniscorthy Rural District Council to build cottages under the Labourers Acts.
	October	Loan of £5,390 raised from Commissioners of Public Works by Wexford Rural District Council to build cottages under the Labourers Acts.
	October	Loan of £579 raised from Commissioners of Public Works by Gorey Rural District Council to build cottages under the Labourers Acts.
	11 December	Sir Thomas H Grattan Esmonde presented official seal to county council.
1900	8 January	A Remington No 8 typewriter purchased for county council office from Mr Timpson, Wexford, at a cost of £23.9s.6d.
	9 April	Council contributed £300 to Evicted Tenants Sustentation Fund.
	1 May	The bank book of the county council showed a credit balance of £16,493.17s.0d.
	13 June	After payments made to guardians and district councils of 'the sum necessary to carry on the working of these bodies', the council's bank book showed a credit balance of £4,129.0s.3d.
	13 June	Annual meeting of the council. Rates in the £ for year ending 31 March 1900 (in decimal equivalent):

Enniscorthy Rural District	18p
Gorey Rural District	15p
New Ross District	22p
Wexford Rural District	15p
Rateable valuation of the county	£384,485.

7 December — Resolution of the council to strike a rate of 1/2d in the £ for the purpose of assisting agriculture and technical Instruction in the county.

1901

5 March — The council's resentment at the damage to roads by motor traffic and the resultant costs demonstrated by a resolution that permission to use the roads by members of the Automobile Club of Great Britain and Ireland be prevented by the council as far as possible.

7 March — Lord M Fitzgerald stated that as regards direct labour, he could say that he could see no cheaper way of keeping roads in repair than the present plan whereby the contracts were open to competition and the work was done by people who live along the roads. These men took the contracts and the principal part of their work was done by members of their own families and they used their horses on the work when there is no farm work to be done. If the council went in for direct labour, certainly they might be confident that the labourers would look for higher wages than they were receiving at present and the work would be altogether more expensive. If they took up direct labour they would undoubtedly incur considerable expense.

April — Loan of £14,000 raised from Commissioners of Public Works by Enniscorthy Rural District Council to build cottages under the Labourers Acts.

7 May — Resolution of sympathy with Lady Maurice Fitzgerald on the death of 'our esteemed colleague,' Lord Maurice Fitzgerald.

1902

April — Loan of £105 raised from Commissioners of Public Works by Gorey Rural District Council to build cottages under the Labourers Acts.

April — Loan of £9,500 raised from Commissioners of Public Works by Wexford Rural District Council to build cottages under the Labourers Acts.

April — Loan of £3,240 raised from Commissioners of Public Works by Gorey Rural District Council to build cottages under the Labourers Acts.

1903

Motor Car Act – Registration and Licensing (Ireland) with respect to the use of locomotives and motor cars on highways. Wexford Index Mark = MI.

3 February — Decision taken to install a telephone in council offices.

31 March — By 31 March 1903 the numbers of cottages provided in the different areas, and let at rents of 3p to 4p per week, were:

Wexford Rural District	499
Enniscorthy Rural District	313
New Ross Rural Distirct	160
Gorey Rural District	186
Total	1,158

April   Loan of £200 raised from Commissioners of Public Works by Wexford Rural District Council to build cottages under the Labourers Acts.

April   Loan of £14,180 raised from Commissioners of Public Works by New Ross Rural District Council to build cottages under the Labourers Acts.

8 June   Sir Thomas Grattan Esmonde proposes that the council restores the old place names of Bunclody and Kiltennell to Newtownbarry and Courtown respectively on the grounds that 'it will contribute towards the preservation of Ireland's monuments and help to perpetuate local topography'.

4 August   Resolution of thanks to the chairman for his work in recovering the Irish Gold ornaments from the British Museum and having them transferred to Ireland.

16 October   Extract from minutes of the county council:
THE IRISH GOLD ORNAMENTS
The following letter was read from Sir Thomas H. G. Esmonde, Bart., M.P.,

Dear Mr. Frizelle,

On my return from abroad I find your letter of August 5th, enclosing a copy of a resolution which the County Council has been good enough to pass with regard to the recovery of the Irish Gold Ornaments from the British Museum.

I am deeply indebted to the Council for this resolution, indicative as it is of the interest they have taken in the long contest which has at last been decided in favour of Ireland.

The importance of our victory will be the more appreciated as years roll on when our country with increasing opportunities and under happier conditions realises her rightful position as the centre of the Celtic world and the depository and the guardian of all that is most valuable in Celtic literature and Celtic Art.

Meantime, I hope that no member of the Council will miss the opportunity, when in Dublin, of visiting the collection of Irish gold ornaments in the National Museum in Kildare Street which is now incomparably the finest in existence,

Faithfully yours,

Thomas H. Grattan Esmonde

CHRONOLOGY

VEHICLE REGISTRATION IN COUNTY WEXFORD

Under the Motor Car Act of 1903, Wexford County Council began the tasks of registering motorised vehicles in the county and of issuing registration numbers prefaced with the index mark MI. By 1911 there were just under 200 registered vehicles carrying the MI mark; by 1921 the number of registered vehicles was under one thousand. On 11 June 1921, a party of police raided County Hall and took away its motor registration and driver licensing registers and forms. A Captain McIntosh, who was in charge of the party, stated that, under martial law, the council no longer had power to transact any business under the Motor Registration and Driver Licensing Acts.

What the ultimate fate of these registers was is now a matter of conjecture. It seems unlikely, however, that the council ever recovered them. The earliest surviving vehicle registration book in the council archives dates from 1922 and begins with registration details for MI 1000. This strongly suggests that when the council returned to the task of vehicle registration, it had no way of determining the point at which it had stopped numerically in the issue of licence numbers. Accordingly, it recommenced registration with the first round number its officials knew had not been previously issued, MI 1000.

The following is a list of the names and addresses of early MI-registered vehicle owners. It is taken from *The Irish Motor Directory and Motor Annual 1911-1912*, edited by Henry G Tempest, and is reprinted verbatim.

Wexford County Cars and Cycles

CARS, 88; CYCLES, 61.

No		Car or Bicycle
MI 1	Col. J R Magrath, Bann-a-Boo, Wexford	C
MI 2	Henry Lloyd Meadows, Ballyrane, Killinick	C
MI 3	Henry Lloyd Meadows, Ballyrane, Killinick	C
MI 4	Major Charles Head, Derrylahan, Birr, King's County	C
MI 7	T W Salmon, Hayestown, Wexford	B
MI 8	Frank B Jacob, Rathdowney, Killinick	C
MI 9	Henry Webster, Cliff House, Enniscorthy	B
MI 10	V G Pigott, Glena Terrace, Wexford	C
MI 11	John Richard Blacker, The Bungalow, Kilrane	B
MI 12	Malcolm MacAlpine, Valency House, Eastbury, North Watford	C
MI 14	Joseph Wakefield, William Street, Tullamore	B
MI 15	Rev. T E G Condell, Kilscoran Rectory, Wexford	B
MI 17	R W Hall-Dare, Newtownbarry House, Newtownbarry	C
MI 18	Percy Hedley, Cefn Cold, Uplands, Swansea	C
MI 20	Joseph A Stokes, Fisher Street, Kinsale	C
MI 21	C Horandner, 4 Vernon Street, SCR, Dublin	B
MI 22	Miss E Hawkes Cornock, Little Clonard, Wexford	C
MI 23	Thomas Wm Thompson, Harbour Works, Kilrane	B
MI 24	Rev. Sylvester Cullen CC, Craanford, Gorey	B
MI 25	Cecil Walpole Marsh, Chichester Gardens, Antrim Rd, Belfast	B
MI 26	Myles Sheil, Ballyvergan, Adamstown	B
MI 28	A J P Wise, Belleville Park, Cappoquin, Co. Waterford	C
MI 29	Matthew Hunter, Ulster Bank, Wexford	B
MI 31	Vincent Rochfort, 14 Inchicore Square, Dublin	B
MI 34	Harold Roberts, Abbey Quay, Enniscorthy	B

The registered owner of MI 8 in 1912 was Frank B Jacob, Rathdowney, Killinick. However, the man behind the wheel in this picture (date unknown) has been identified as James J Kirwan, cattle dealer, John Street, Wexford.

The vehicle currently bearing the registration number MI 1 is this De Dion Bouton owned by Osmond Bennett, Johnstown, Co. Kilkenny. Following the Motor Car Act of 1903, motorised vehicles were required to display registration numbers issued by the local licensing authority, the county council. A registration number could be transferred to another vehicle in certain circumstances, e.g. if the original vehicle had been scrapped, or sold outside the county of registration. The registered owner of MI 1 c. 1912 was Colonel J R Magrath, Bann-a-boo, Wexford. In 1897, Colonel Magrath owned an Arnold which he had imported from England. A list of seventeen cars in County Wexford in 1904 describes the vehicle owned by Colonel Magrath as a 7hp Turrell. However, it is not clear which, if any, of these vehicles was first registered as MI 1. In 1922, according to the council's vehicle registration books, the registration number MI 1 was assigned to an 18hp dark green Ford owned by J C Beauchamp Doran of Ely House, Wexford. The council also issued garage plates and the first one, MI 0001, was, by 1922, owned by R H Nixon, Gorey, Co. Wexford.

MI	35	Wm Thorpe, Knockroe, New Ross	B
MI	36	Rev. M Hickey CC, Templeudigan, Ballywilliam	B
MI	37	Dr William J Shee, Bella Vista, Duncannon	B
MI	38	Harry G Tempest, Douglas Place, Dundalk	B
MI	39	George Reginald Moody, Rathaspeck, Wexford	B
MI	40	Richard A Rice, Ballygarvan, New Ross	B
MI	42	Edward Meadows, Bushville, Killinick	C
MI	43	Granville MacAlpine, Balloughton House, Bannow	B
MI	45	Thomas J Kelly, Slaney Place, Enniscorthy	C
MI	46	Thomas Malcolm MacAlpine, Balloughton House, Bannow	C
MI	50	Edward Slator McDonald, The Cottage, Wellingtonbridge	B
MI	51	Michael Breen, Rock Factory, Enniscorthy	B
MI	55	George M Link, Four Courts Hotel, Dublin	B
MI	56	John Carroll, North Street, New Ross	B
MI	57	Frederick Hughes, Upton House, Kilmuckridge	C
MI	58	Rev. Francis Moran, The Manse, Newtownbarry	B
MI	62	Robert O'Leary, 10 Georges Street, Enniscorthy	B
MI	63	T Malcolm MacAlpine, Balloughton House, Bannow	C
MI	64	Edward Cavanagh, St John's, Enniscorthy	B

MI 66	F P Roche, Woodville, New Ross	B
MI 67	Herbert Thompson, Quay, Wexford	B
MI 68	P L K Dobbin, County Surveyor, Ennis, Co. Clare	B
MI 69	Myles Sheil, Ballyvergan, Adamstown	B
MI 72	Thomas J Dowse MD, George Street, Wexford	C
MI 73	Wm R Telford, Garrymore, Clara, King's County	C
MI 74	Rev. Francis Moran, The Manse, Newtownbarry	B
MI 75	A W Harty, Garryowen House, Limerick	B
MI 77	Dr M W Kelly, Larkfield, Kilann	B
MI 78	A J H Meadows, Thornville, Ballycogley	C
MI 79	B A W Lett, Ballyvergan, Adamstown	C
MI 80	F C Hamlyn Brown, The Bungalow, Arklow	B
MI 83	Anthony Convey, Templeshannon, Enniscorthy	C
MI 84	Hugh McGuire, Main Street, Wexford	B
MI 86	Wm J Neil, The Cottage, Greenmount, Harold's Cross, Dublin	B
MI 88	R E Hall, Park View, Gorey	B
MI 89	T M McAlpine, Wellington Bridge, Wexford	C
MI 91	J J Aird, Maryboro', Queen's County	C
MI 92	Henry S Tyndall, Ballyanne House, New Ross	B
MI 93	Anthony Loftus Cliffe, Bellevue, Wexford	C
MI 94	Joseph M Ronan, George Street, Wexford	C
MI 95	Louis C Tree, 6 New Square, Lincoln Inn, London, WC	B
MI 96	Capt. Loftus A Bryan, Borrmount Manor, Enniscorthy	Q
MI 99	Henry J Roche, Cliff House, Enniscorthy	B
MI 100	George E V Cuppage, Clare Hall, Raheny, Co. Dublin	C
MI 102	H J Meldrum, Manchester Road, Altrisham	C
MI 104	Thomas Thompson & Son Ltd, 15 Talbot Place, Dublin	C
MI 105	George Phillips RIC, Cullingtree Road, Belfast	B
MI 106	Stafford Gaffney, Richmond Terrace, Wexford	C
MI 107	Rev. T E Condell, Kilscoran Rectory, Wexford	B
MI 110	George Heaton, 47 Newhall Street, Birmingham	C
MI 111	Milbrowe Smith, 7 Grove Lane, Handsworth, Birmingham	C
MI 112	Dr W J Shee, Bella Vista, Duncannon	B

R to L: Lady Maurice Fitzgerald, Captain Ronald Forbes, chauffeur William Breslin, and Geraldine Fitzgerald pose in Lady Maurice's Dixi car, registration number MI 135 at Johnstown Castle c. 1910. Dixi cars were manufactured in Eisenach, Germany, from 1904 until 1928. The company was then acquired by BMW.

A Merryweather Fire Engine c.1929, once the property of Wexford Corporation, now in private ownership.

MI 113	A R Browne, 21 Court Street, Enniscorthy	B
MI 114	Col. J H Newman, Ballyrankin, Ferns	C
MI 115	G H Jack, Shirehall, Hereford	C
MI 116	H T Cooke, The Arcade, Gorey	B
MI 117	A Constantine, The Anchorage, Handsworth Wood, Staff	C
MI 118	Francis Rutledge, Coolbawn Cottage, Enniscorthy	C
MI 119	John Noblett, Ballinastraw, Clonegal	B
MI 120	P A Jeffares, New Ross	B
MI 121	Rev. Wm R B Fry, The Rectory, Newtownbarry	C
MI 123	Henry Woodroofe, Glandoran, Gorey	B
MI 124	Malachy Scally, William Street, Tullamore	C
MI 125	R H Nixon, 42 Main Street, Gorey	B
MI 126	C R Boyse, Millpark House, Enniscorthy	C
MI 127	Rev. J Redmond, Ferns	B
MI 128	R H Nixon, 42 Main Street, Gorey	B
MI 129	Thomas A Whitney, Killanne	B
MI 130	Major A W M Richards, Ardamine, Gorey	C
MI 131	Myles Sheill, Cullentra, Wexford	C
MI 132	Henry Corkery, 3 Martello Terrace, Kingstown	C
MI 133	F J Walsh, Crescent Quay, Wexford	C
MI 135	Lady M Fitzgerald, Johnstown Castle, Wexford	C
MI 136	J F Hug, Falmouth House, Wilde Green, Birmingham	C
MI 137	R P Mulholland, 5 High Croft Road, Hornsey Rise, London	C
MI 138	R F Spring, Polihore, Wexford	C
MI 139	Rev. P Doyle, Rathnew	C
MI 140	Rev. J Ashton, Ardamine Rectory, Gorey	C
MI 142	Joseph Barber, 28 Corn Market, Belfast	B
MI 143	Patrick J Roche, Woodville, New Ross	C

MI 144	John Pierce, Park House, Wexford	C
MI 145	John M Roche, Knockmullin, New Ross	C
MI 146	Robert W Hall-Dare, Newtownbarry Ho, Newtownbarry	C
MI 147	H T A S Boyce, Bannow, Co Wexford	C
MI 148	Juliet M Lavie, Newlands, Ferns	C
MI 149	Dr D Hadden Jun., Lower George Street, Wexford	C
MI 150	Wm B Nunn, Castlebridge, Co. Wexford	C
MI 152	Edward Hartrick, Robinstown, Palace	B
MI 153	Denis J Nolan, Munster & Leinster Bank, New Ross	C
MI 154	H T Buckland, 21 Yateley Road, Edgbaston, Birmingham	C
MI 155	Dr Wm C Lawler, Riverview, Newtownbarry	C
MI 156	James Walsh, Danescastle, Bannow	B
MI 157	F P Roche, The Castle, Enniscorthy	C
MI 158	Edward G H Gardner, Danesway, Circencester, Gloster	C
MI 159	P C Alcock, Wilton Castle, Enniscorthy	C
MI 160	Richard Whitney, Main Street, Gorey	C
MI 161	Harold C Hughes, Lapworth Grange, Warwickshire	C
MI 162	M V McKevitt, Kilkerley Cottage, Dundalk	B
MI 163	C G Nicol, Fernville, Gorey	C
MI 164	Henry J Roche, The Castle, Enniscorthy	C
MI 166	Philip C Alcock, Wilton Castle, Enniscorthy	B
MI 167	Charles E Barton, Ruane, New Ross	C
MI 168	Ivor Francis Chichester, Rosepark, Wexford	C
MI 169	Messrs Thompson Bros, Custom House Quay, Wexford	B
MI 170	Messrs Philip Pierce & Co., Wexford	C
MI 172	Patrick W Murphy, Kilraine, Wexford	B
MI 173	Francis Wm Davis, Ballinabarna, Enniscorthy	C
MI 174	Wm Wentworth Murphy, Coolgreany, Inch, Co. Wexford	B
MI 175	Wm B Nunn, Castlebridge, Wexford	C
MI 176	Frank Edward Bailey, 63 Grove Lane, Handsworth, Staffs	C
MI 177	Mrs Laura Chadwick, Minto Hall, Tamworth	C
MI 178	Messrs Thompson Bros, Custom House Quay, Wexford	C
MI 179	Wm J Doyle VS, Templeshannon, Enniscorthy	C
MI 180	Richard Henry Nixon, 42 Main Street, Gorey	C
MI 181	Mrs Maud Dawson, Palace, New Ross	C
MI 182	Rev. John Rowe, Kilmore Quay, Wexford	C
MI 183	Pierre Goffette, White's Hotel, Wexford	C
MI 184	James Taylor, Market Square, Enniscorthy	C
MI 185	Richard F Spring, Polehore Glynn, Wexford	C
MI 186	Major Lewis M Dunbar, Upton, Kilmuckridge	C
MI 187	Thomas Cogley, Killurin, Wexford	B
MI 188	Wm Hillock, 1 George's Street, Enniscorthy	B
MI 189	Anthony Loftus Bryan, Carrigmannon, Wexford	T
MI 190	Thomas L Esmonde, Ballycourcy, Enniscorthy	C
MI 192	S A Furlong, Infirmary House, Wexford	B
MI 193	Bates & Sons, Gorey	C

1904	April	Loan of £850 raised from Commissioners of Public Works by Gorey Rural District Council to build cottages under the Labourers Acts.
1905	April	Loan of £18,000 raised from Commissioners of Public Works by Enniscorthy Rural District Council to build cottages under the Labourers Acts.
	April	Loan of £17,000 raised from the Treasurer by Wexford Rural District Council to build cottages under the Labourers Acts.
	April	Loan of £5,000 raised from Commissioners of Public Works by Enniscorthy Rural District Council to build cottages under the Labourers Acts.
	16 September	Wexford Jail premises handed over to Wexford County Council, the successors in title to the County Wexford Grand Jury.
1907	25 January	The application of the secretary to have a metaphone connection between the county surveyor's office and the county secretary's office was approved.
1908	13 June	Staff of county council granted holidays as follows: county surveyor, 1 month; county secretary, 3 weeks; clerical staff, 2 weeks, 'to be taken as the exigencies of official work permit'.
1909	4 May	Agreement with Sisters of St John of God for use of the old jail property as a rehabilitation home under the name St Brigid's Inebriate Home.
1910		Finance Act – imposition of a duty upon motor cars extended to Ireland.
1911	April	Loan of £24,263 raised from Irish Land Commission by Wexford Rural District Council to build cottages under the Labourers Acts.
	April	Loan of £500 raised from Irish Land Commission by New Ross Rural District Council to build cottages under the Labourers Acts.
	April	Loan of £2,000 raised from Irish Land Commission by Wexford Rural District Council to build cottages under the Labourers Acts.
	April	Loan of £200 raised from Irish Land Commission by Wexford Rural District Council to build cottages under the Labourers Acts.
	April	Loan of £13,000 raised from Irish Land Commission by New Ross Rural District Council to build cottages under the Labourers Acts.
	April	Loan of £1,500 raised from Irish Land Commission by Gorey Rural District Council to build cottages under the Labourers Acts.
	13 April	Seal of county council affixed to the deed investing the Windmill on Vinegar Hill, Enniscorthy, in the county council. The Windmill was ceded to the council by its owners,

CHRONOLOGY

1912
Anastatia Maguire and her son, Thomas.
Killurin bridge begins construction.

31 March By 31 March 1912 the numbers of cottages provided in the different areas, and let at rents of 3p to 11p per week, were:

Wexford Rural District	843
Enniscorthy Rural District	541
New Ross Rural Distirct	312
Gorey Rural District	287
Total	1,983

1913

April Loan of £6,000 raised from Irish Land Commission by Wexford Rural District Council to build cottages under the Labourers Acts.

April Loan of £8,000 raised from Irish Land Commission by Gorey Rural District Council to build cottages under the Labourers Acts.

April Loan of £6,200 raised from Irish Land Commission by Gorey Rural District Council to build cottages under the Labourers Acts.

April Loan of £2,000 raised from Irish Land Commission by New

Order signed by Secretary N J Frizelle and drawn on the council's Treasurer, the National Bank, in payment of £2. 9s. 0d. to Denis Dempsey, Blackwater for 'maintenance of a road', 1912.

The newly-constructed Killurin Bridge c. 1914.

		Ross Rural District Council to build cottages under the Labourers Acts.
	April	Loan of £1,000 raised from Irish Land Commission by Gorey Rural District Council to build cottages under the Labourers Acts.
	April	Loan of £250 raised from Irish Land Commission by New Ross Rural District Council to build cottages under the Labourers Acts.
	April	Loan of £4,050 raised from Irish Land Commission by Gorey Rural District Council to build cottages under the Labourers Acts.
	April	Loan of £4,000 raised from Irish Land Commission by New Ross Rural District Council to build cottages under the Labourers Acts.
	April	Loan of £130 raised from Irish Land Commission by Wexford Rural District Council to build cottages under the Labourers Acts.
	7 May	County surveyor reported on the repairs necessary to render Wexford Free Bridge safe for traffic, excluding traction engines, for 12 years. Estimated cost of repair – £4,000. County surveyor recommended a new bridge opposite the courthouse at an estimated cost of £37,360. Consideration postponed for two years.
1915	April	Loan of £43,500 raised from Irish Land Commission by Enniscorthy Rural District Council to build cottages under the Labourers Acts.
1916	April	Loan of £1,500 raised from Irish Land Commission by Wexford Rural District Council to build cottages under the Labourers Acts.
	April	Loan of £2,000 raised from Irish Land Commission by Gorey Rural District Council to build cottages under the Labourers Acts.

The Recent Disturbances.

On the motion of Mr Kehoe, seconded by Sir Tho[mas]
Standing Orders of the Council were suspended to enable [...]
move a resolution.

The Chairman then moved the following resolu[tion]

"That we deplore the lamentable rising in [...]
which occurred during Easter week. Particularly in [...]
when the loss of life and property has been appalli[ng]

We firmly believe that this Criminal rebell[ion]
by Germany to promote her own selfish ends.

That we believe many young men that took p[art]
idea of the foolishness of their action and were [...]
such criminal folly.

We therefore call on Mr Redmond and our [...]
ment to use their influence with the Government [...]
young men who are now prisoners.

That we hereby renew our entire confi[dence]
the Irish Party, and assure them of our unswe[rving]

Mr Kinsella seconded the resolution, which [...]
T. Esmonde, and Mr Kehoe.

The resolution was adopted unanimously.

	April	Loan of £1,500 raised from Irish Land Commission by Gorey Rural District Council to build cottages under the Labourers Acts.
	April	Loan of £1,500 raised from Irish Land Commission by New Ross Rural District Council to build cottages under the Labourers Acts.
	April	Loan of £4,510 raised from Bank of Ireland, Gorey, by Gorey Rural District Council to build cottages under the Labourers Acts.
	17 May	County surveyor reported that he had been directed by the county inspector of the RIC to make St Brigid's Home suitable for the reception of prisoners.
1917	April	Loan of £355 raised from Irish Land Commission by Gorey Rural District Council to build cottages under the Labourers Acts.
	5 December	Superintendent of St Brigid's Home gave notice of the intended closure and replacement with accommodation for children suffering from mental handicap.
1918	April	Loan of £5,050 raised from Bank of Ireland, Gorey, by Gorey Rural District Council to build cottages under the Labourers Acts.
	April	Loan of £220 raised from Irish Land Commission by Gorey Rural District Council to build cottages under the Labourers Acts.

		Loan of £1,330 raised from Irish Land Commission by Gorey Rural District Council to build cottages under the Labourers Acts.
	June	First election to the council under proportional representation system.
	18 June	County council acknowledges authority of Dáil Éireann as 'duly elected government for the Irish people'.
	18 June	Resolutions passed by the council in 1915 and 1916 (advocating recruitment to the British army and condemning the Easter Rising) were rescinded.
	August	Agreement with the Sisters of St John of God for surrender of old jail property.
	2 September	Last meeting of the council held in the Courthouse, The Quay, Wexford.
	7 October	First meeting of the council in the old jail premises, described as the 'County Hall'.
	7 October	Motion adopted that the name of Newtownbarry be changed to the old Gaelic form, *Bun Cloidighe*.
	22 November	Books and records removed from county council offices by a party of Royal Irish Constabulary.
1921	January	New scheme for the registration and licensing of mechanically propelled vehicles comes into force. County council reestablished as the licensing authority under the provisions of the Finance and Roads Acts 1920.
	11 January	Rate collectors complain that their collecting books have been seized by 'armed and masked men'.
	April	Loan of £3,700 raised from Irish Land Commission by Gorey

After Wexford County Council declared allegiance to Dáil Éireann on 18 June 1920 it was effectively deemed illegal for the purposes of collecting rates by the Local Government Board. This created a dilemma for the rate collectors who had been appointed by the council and to which they had given sureties. The Board issued frequent notices to the ratepayers advising them against paying rates to the council's agents.

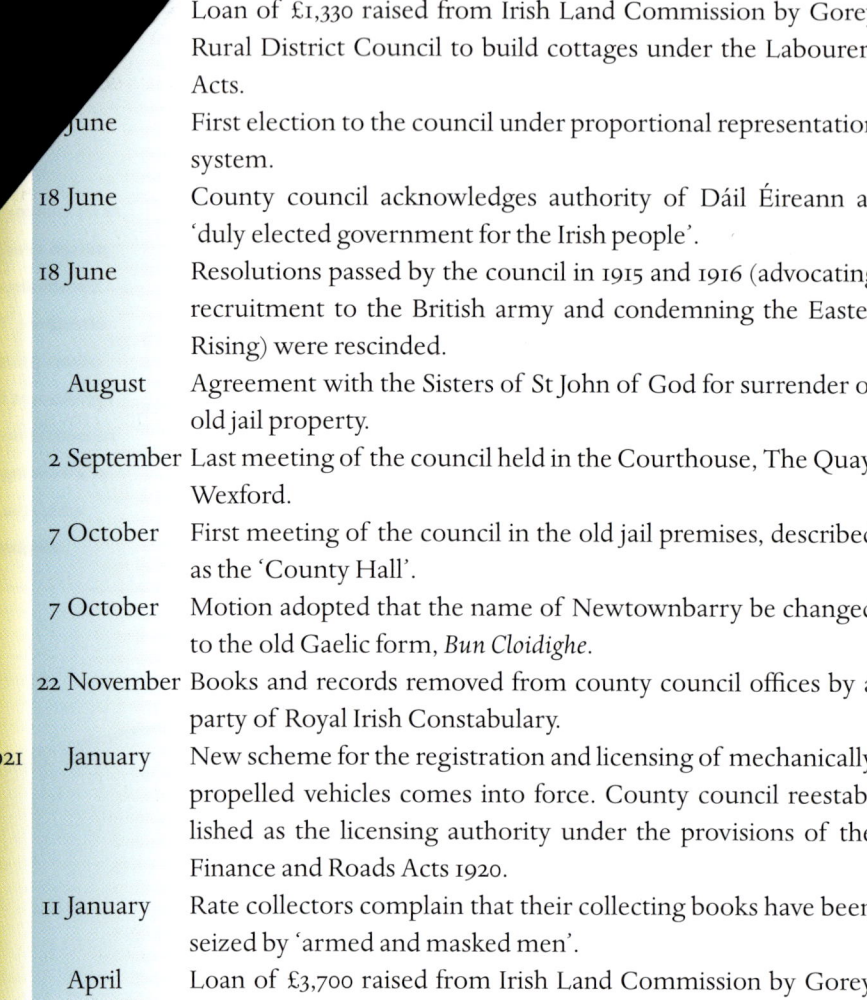

CHRONOLOGY

	Rural District Council to build cottages under the Labourers Acts.
11 June	County council's motor registration and driver licensing registers and forms confiscated by RIC.
18 June	Courthouse destroyed by explosion and fire.
4 July	County Hall commandeered by the RIC for use as a concentration depot prior to their disbandment. County Council headquarters moved to a disused ward in the Wexford Workhouse.
14 July	First meeting of the council in temporary accommodation in the Wexford Workhouse.
4 October	First meeting of the county council in the Town Hall, Wexford, by courtesy of the mayor in view of the inadequacy of the accommodation for such meetings in the Wexford Workhouse.
1922/3	Carnegie Trust initiated experimental library scheme in Co. Wexford. First centre opened in Riverchapel.
1922 13 March	County secretary informed the council that the RIC evacuated the County Hall on 11 March 1922.
3 April	Council meetings resumed in the County Hall after evacuation by the RIC.
30 June	Portion of County Hall made available for use of circuit court.
31 July	County surveyor reported on damaged roads and bridges. He said:

> In some cases the damage was repaired and has since been re-damaged. In a number of cases where I have endeavoured to get men to attend to this repair work they have refused and I consider that a further endeavour to make good the damage at the present time will be of no avail owing to the fact that any repair work is immediately undone if not prevented from being carried out.
>
> With regard to bridge on 3R (New Ross) I had myself arranged for its repair and the work was put in hand the following day but was destroyed on completion. Also the bridge on 24W (Wexford), I inspected it on Wednesday evening and was arranging with regard to making good the roadway but I am informed today that further damage has been done by blast last night.
>
> With regard to the County-at-large Bridges over Slaney and Barrow Rivers, I have given you all particulars of their present condition and I consider any temporary repairs now would be absolutely worthless unless a guard can be put on the structures.

| 16 October | Attempt to burn the County Hall. The secretary reported: |

Nora Connolly, County Librarian 1928-1967.

On the night of the 16th October, between eight and nine p.m. the County Hall was raided by a number of armed men, some of whom held up the Caretaker in his kitchen at revolver point. They set fire to the central hall, in which were all books of account, ledgers etc., for the past three years, using some gallons of petrol for the purpose. As soon as they left the building the matter was reported to the military who extinguished the fire. Fortunately, the damage to the hall is slight but the books are entirely destroyed.

1923	5 February	County Hall taken over by the military. The following report was submitted by the secretary:

> I beg to report that on the 23rd January, 1923, the County Hall premises were inspected by General Mulcahy and Major-General McMahon.
> … General Mulcahy informed me that the military intended to take over the premises, that time would be allowed to the County Council to transfer their property …

At a meeting on 12 March 1923 the following letter from Lt Comdt Liam McGaffney was read:

> Please take notice that I, on behalf of the National Army, will take possession of County Hall on Monday, 5th day of March. You will have all goods, chattels, papers etc., the property of the County Council, removed before that date.

	5 March	Council headquarters moved to newly acquired premises in Fortview, Spawell Road, Wexford.
	9 April	First meeting of the council in the boardroom at Fortview, Spawell Road, Wexford.
1924	30 October	Surrender of County Hall by military. The following was submitted from minutes of Finance and Roads Committee meeting:

> Under date 25th October, 1924, Comdt. McNally, Command Quartermaster, Eastern Command, Collins Barracks, Dublin, wrote (No.ECQ/504) that the military authorities proposed to hand back to the County Council the premises known as Wexford Jail (County Hall). Comdt. McRory and a representative from the Board of Works would attend at the Jail on the 30th October, 1924, at 12 o'clock for the purpose of handing over the premises to someone acting on behalf of the Council.

The following recommendation was adopted on the motion of Mr O'Byrne, seconded by Mr Hayes:

> That the County Surveyor be appointed to take over from the military authorities on the 30th October, 1924, the County Hall. The surrender to be accepted without prejudice to all claims of all kinds and description on behalf of the Council in connection with the premises while out of their control.

1925 Under section 65 of Local Government Act, Wexford County Council becomes the library authority for the county. A rate of a halfpenny in the pound is levied for library purposes for the financial year 1925-26.

29 May Under date 29 May 1925 Colonel Mitchel, Secretary to the Carnegie United Kingdom Trust, wrote that Wexford County Council, having resolved to undertake the responsibility for the Wexford Rural Library Service, and to provide adequate sums for maintenance from public funds, the Carnegie United Kingdom Trustees had agreed to hand over the assets and to transfer the entire administration of the library service to the county council as from 1 April 1925.

16 June On the motion of the chairman, seconded by Mr Cloney the following resolution was adopted:

> That the following be appointed as County Library Committee to carry on the work of the library until the new committee has been appointed:
> Messrs T Lungley
> D Whelan
> P Hickey
> J F Heffernan
> Rev. R Fitzhenry
> Miss N O'Ryan
> Miss Verney.

23 July Department of Local Government and Public Health advised county councils that financial control should be retained by the parent bodies over committees established under the Local Government Act 1925 and unprofitable expenditure of time on minor matters of administration should be avoided. Perpetuation, through numerous local committees of the old system of rural administration should be avoided. Local committees should be purely advisory.

14 September The council was informed that the Automobile Association was prepared to provide direction signs in the places indicated by the council provided the latter undertake their erection.

14 September The council was informed that the maximum laden weight for

		a 'heavy motor car' to be licensed in future was nine tons (rather than twelve tons as hitherto).
	14 September	The county surveyor reported that a council employee working on the rolling scheme at Ferrycarrig Road had been accidentally killed but the cause of his death was outside his proper work. (The accident resulted from a good-humoured exchange between the employee and a passer-by.)
1926	11 January	Minutes of the council meeting at page 334 list the main roads declared by the minister under the Local Government Act 1925. Effective 1 April 1926.
	11 January	Resolution of the council that 'in view of the injury to a large number of roads in this county resulting from heavy lorry traffic, we request the government to limit same to six tons all-in and that no trailers be allowed'.
	22 February	The council adopted a rate in the £ of 44p on buildings and 31p on land (allowing for the effect of the Agricultural Grant).
	8 March	All cottages, plots and gardens provided by the boards of guardians and rural district councils under the Labourers Acts, which had become the property of the county council, transferred to the County Board of Health.
	12 April	At the request of District Justice O Fathaigh the council agreed to the use of the council chamber at Fortview for a sitting of the district court in view of dissatisfaction with the temporary facilities provided since the burning of the courthouse. Temporary use of 'the first room on the left as one enters the old Jail premises' as an office for the district court clerk was also approved.
	10 May	Council adopted a resolution that the speed of 'heavy motor cars' crossing New Ross Bridge be restricted to three miles per hour and that the solicitor be instructed to prepare the relevant by-law.
	10 May	Extract from council minutes:

> The County Surveyor considered, relative to the use of the old Jail premises, that if the £5000 compensation awarded by the Government were expended on the buildings, a sufficiently good Courthouse and County Council Office could be secured at the old Jail.
>
> Owing to the fact that the Local Government had cut down the amount to be spent at the old Courthouse from £13,000 to £10,000, it would not be possible to secure on the site of the old Courthouse the extra accommodation that would be required by the Council.
>
> Col. Gibbon proposed that, as a Committee had already seen these buildings and had, on the advice of the Architect Mr. Delap and the County Surveyor,

turned down any proposals for these repairs, it was advisable that an unprejudiced Committee of the Council went into the matter anew and made a report to the County Council.

Mr Boggan seconded.

Passed.

27 May First sitting of the circuit court in the County Hall. The council provided temporary accommodation in the chapel of the old jail at the request of the clerk of the peace.

14 June The county surveyor reported that up to the present he had provided for erection of 117 sign posts covering the main roads of the county and he awaited the delivery of the direction signs by the Automobile Association.

14 June The following report was received from the county surveyor:

> As directed by the Council I transferred the fittings from the old Courthouse on the Quay to the Chapel at the old Jail and have fitted it up as a Circuit Court which is at present sitting. The furniture from the New Ross Workhouse has been brought to Wexford and is at present in the old Jail premises. A good deal of this furniture was of great utility in fitting up the premises as a Courthouse.

23 August Special meeting of the council to recommend whether work on the Enniscorthy-Wexford road under a grant of £36,976 should be carried out by direct labour or by contract.

The council recommended direct labour but the decision finally was to surface the road in concrete using experienced contractors.

13 September Council resolved to ask the Minister for Local Government and Public Health to prohibit the driving of 'heavy motor cars' at a speed exceeding 3 miles per hour on New Ross Bridge, motor cars at a speed exceeding 10 miles per hour on Wexford Bridge and motor cars at a speed exceeding 15 miles per hour on the road from Gorey to Courtown Harbour.

30 September Plan for renovation of the old jail as a courthouse and for county offices at an estimated cost of £4,097 submitted by the county surveyor.

3 October District engineers and gangers directed to release roads staff for emergency saving of corn crops, the council to pay the wages of the men concerned.

11 October Council ask for reason Department of Local Government and Public Health decided to have the work on the Wexford-Enniscorthy road done by contract rather than direct labour.

Mr Boggan mentioned that in his opinion it was a misapplication of the grant to construct roads for the use of heavy lorries.

	11 October	Council informed by the Department of Local Government and Public Health that because the council did not have sufficient relevant experience to do the work by direct labour it had been decided to do so by contract.
1927	28 February	Tender of Pioneer Roads Construction Company, East Wall, Drumcondra, Dublin, at £39,424 for reconstruction of Wexford-Enniscorthy road accepted.

Contract will provide for a concrete surface, 12 foot wide, which Mr Quigley from the Department of Local Government and Public Health expected would last for twelve to twenty years without requiring serious work. |
| | 9 May | The council informed that the minister had made an order fixing speed limits of
    (a) 3 miles per hour for heavy motor cars proceeding over New Ross Bridge
    (b) 10 miles per hour for motor cars proceeding over Wexford Bridge, and
    (c) 15 miles per hour for motor cars proceeding along the road from Gorey to Courtown Harbour. |
	4 July	The council was informed that the joint committee with Kilkenny County Council to oversee the building of the new bridge at Ferrymountgarret had provisionally accepted the tender of John Hearn and Son, Waterford, for construction of the bridge for the sum of £18,839. (Estimated all-in cost £22,750 to which the Department of Local Government and Public Health would contribute 25% and the two county councils £8,530 each.)
1928	January	Resignation of Josephine Walsh, county librarian. Eileen Doyle, Tagoat, appointed as acting county librarian for February and March.
	April	Appointment of Nora Connolly as county librarian.
	10 December	The county surveyor informed the council that of 1,968 miles of road in the county 103 miles were classified as trunk roads and 194 miles as link roads. Grant aid for upkeep of trunk roads for 1929 would be at the rate of 50% and link roads at 30%. About 69 miles of trunk roads had been dealt with but nothing had been done with link roads.
1929	25 February	The Estimate of Expenses for the year 1929-30 was adopted and a general rate of 40p in the £ on buildings and 28p in the £ on land was determined.

The estimates provided for Public Assistance Services £58,000, Board of Health £70,000 and County Council Services £55,400. |
| | 9 December | Invitations to tender for reconstruction of old jail to be advertised. |
| 1930 | | First report of Wexford County Rural Library Service produced. |

CHRONOLOGY

		It showed there were 64 adult and 43 juvenile centres in the county. 1,654 volumes had been puchased during the financial year ending 31 March 1930, bringing the total stock to 11,117. Total issues from library centres: 41,347
1931	23 March	Council meetings resumed in County Hall after headquarters transferred from Fortview.
	April	Loan of £9,000 raised from Royal Liver Friendly Society to build cottages at Garden City, Gorey.
1932	29 March	Motion to renovate right wing of County Hall to house HQ of Wexford Rural Library Service.
1933		Library headquarters transferred from Custom House Quay, Wexford, to County Hall.
	April	Loan of £1,294 raised from Commissioners of Public Works to complete cottages at Garden City, Gorey.
	9 May	Loan of £1,600 raised fron OPW for housing in Gorey Garden City.
	7 June	Loan of £123,000 raised from OPW for 500 houses (484 built).
	22 June	Plans for reconstruction of the 'West Wing' of the old jail sanctioned by the Minister for Local Government and Public Health.
	14 August	Loan of £8,000 raised from OPW to provide house purchase and building loans.
	6 November	Large room in the west wing [of the old jail] now under reconstruction to be used as the council chamber.
1934	14 December	Loan of £10,000 raised from OPW to provide house purchase and building loans.
1935	9 April	Loan of £12,000 raised from OPW for 56 houses (53 built).
1936	14 April	Loan of £7,000 raised from OPW for Enniscorthy Vocational School.
	28 July	Loan of £34,500 raised from OPW for 115 houses in Ferns, Bunclody and Rosslare Harbour.
	14 December	Loan of £10,000 raised from OPW to provide house purchase and building loans.
	22 December	Loan of £52,000 raised from OPW for 208 houses (204 built).
1937	20 November	Loan of £52,800 raised from OPW for 176 houses (165 built).
1938	11 February	Loan of £43,900 raised from OPW for 129 houses (112 built).
1939	3 April	Supplementary loan of £13,600 raised from OPW for 176 house scheme (see 1937).
	4 April	Loan of £4,015 raised from OPW for 11 houses in Taghmon.
	12 April	Supplementary loan of £7,500 raised from OPW for 115 house scheme (see 1936).
1940	29 January	Loan of £35,040 raised from OPW for 96 houses (74 built).
1941	13 January	County council approved of employment of assessors for competition for Wexford Bridge.
	8 February	Loan of £3,830 raised from OPW for work on St Senan's Hospital, Enniscorthy.

	24 February	Loan of £3,400 raised from OPW for County Hospital site.
	9 July 1941	Loan of £21,600 raised from OPW for 60 houses.
	28 July 1941	Loan of £18,000 raised (£10,300 drawn) from OPW for 47 houses (18 built).
1942	25 November	Loan of £1,875 raised from OPW for work on District and Fever Hospitals.
	4 December	Loan of £3,800 raised from OPW for 10 houses at Kilmuckridge.
1943	31 March	Revenue Expenditure for Year – £223,227. Capital Expenditure for Year – £18,876.
	16 July	Rent of cottages erected in Hollyfort and Neemstown Village scheme to be fixed at 2s (10p) per week exclusive of rates.
	21 July	Employment of sheep dipping inspectors in Enniscorthy, Gorey and New Ross Districts with remuneration of £2.50 per week approved.
	23 July	Approval given to a new road from Ramsfort Park Road, Gorey, to Gorey Garden City Road at a cost not exceeding £100.
	16 August	Work to prevent further erosion at Courtown Harbour in accordance with plans prepared by Nicholas O'Dwyer, Consulting Engineer, approved.
	20 August	Proposed new bridge at Wexford. County Manager approved the conditions for a competition for the design of a bridge over the River Slaney at Wexford. Premia in the conditions are:- Author of the design placed first by the assessors – £500 Author of the design placed second by the assessors – £300 Author of the design placed third by the assessors – £200.
	15 September	Price of £3 per ton, ex bog, fixed for turf produced from Moneer Bog.
	24 September	Approval given to fees payable to Wexford Corporation for the service of the Fire Brigade at incidents in the Wexford County Health District (the rural area).
	24 September	Planting of trees on road margins. Approval given to quotation of Galvin Brothers, Wexford, for supplying apple trees (3-year, half standard) at £18.75 per hundred for planting on road margins throughout the county.
1943	29 September	Approval given to supply of provisions to hospitals in Wexford, New Ross and Gorey, including bread at 5p per 4 lbs loaf, beef at 6p per lb, mutton at 7.5p per lb.
	11 October	Gorey Volunteer Fire Brigade: approval given to organisation and payments for services – Joseph Hobbs, vice-captain, to be responsible for care and maintenance of the trailer pump, for mobilisation of the Fire Brigade, keeping records and organising twelve practices of the brigade annually and for the custody of clothing and equipment. Retention in the brigade

		made conditional on regular and punctual attendance. Payment by way of honorarium – 10p to 12.5p per hour, maximum 75p per callout.
	25 October	Letting of county council traction engines for threshing purposes: approval to a scheme for the hire of council traction engines during the threshing season 1943-44 to approved persons. Hirer to pay £6 per week for the engine plus £3 for driver and supply fuel, oil and water.
	23 November	Purchase of supplementary equipment for Bunclody Fire Brigade approved.
	15 December	Sealing of mortgage to National Bank Ltd, to secure loan of £6,000 for preliminary expenses of Wexford New Bridge approved.
1944	9 February	Price of turf from Moneer Bog supplied to the various county institutions fixed at prices between £2.98 and £3.23 per ton.
	29 March	Tender of William Lee, Arklow, accepted on the recommendation of P H McCarthy, consulting engineer, for the construction of sewage works at Courtown for the sum of £4,677.65.
	29 March	Appointment of Mr Thomas Kelly, Mount Brilliant Road, Kilkenny, as county engineer approved on the recommendation of the Local Appointments Commission.
	31 March	The number of houses provided by the council up to this date, under the enabling legislation, was 3,626.
	31 March	Tenants appointed to 12 houses in the Castlebridge Village scheme.
	31 March	Revenue Expenditure for Year – £328,790. Capital Expenditure for Year – £13,214.
	17 April	Retirement of N J Frizelle, county secretary, on reaching the age limit for the office, noted.
	5 June	Wexford County Council resolved that the sum of £419, representing the produce of a rate of one fourth of one penny, be allocated as a contribution towards the maintenance of Wexford Harbour as an ex gratia payment to meet emergency conditions.
	17 July	Approval to trial holes in the suggested site for new burial ground at Oulart.
	18 July	110 applications for seed loans to a total amount of £1,569 were approved.
	28 July	Formal approval given to the transfer of officers of the Wexford County Board of Health to the same or analogous positions in the Wexford County Council. Officers included Nicholas Kehoe, Aidan A Connolly, Laurence O'Mahoney, Brendan Corish, Miss Ellen Hore.
	17 August	Tender of John Redmond for cutting of corn on mental hospital farm at 57.5p per acre was accepted.

District Hospital, Gorey.

	18 August	In view of communication from the Department of Industry and Commerce under date 4 August 1944, it was agreed that local farmers be allowed remove limited quantities of sand from Rosslare Strand, the concession to remain in operation for one year and the maximum amount removed not to exceed 500 tons.
	23 August	The Minister for Local Government and Publlic Health was requested, for the conveniece of public administration, to change the name of Newtownbarry District Electoral Division to *Bun Cloidighe* District Electoral Division.
	29 August	The application of two ambulance drivers at New Ross for alternate Sundays off duty was granted, the matter to be reconsidered at the end of six months.
	29 August	Employment of two temporary engineers at remuneration of £6.30 per week for three months for preparation of surveys and plans under emergency schemes and post-war planning arrangements approved.
	4 September	Approval was given to a new 250-year lease of New Ross Courthouse from 1 July 1944 at the yearly rent of £45.
	18 October	The resurfacing in concrete of William Street and Trinity Street, Wexford, from Unemployment Relief Grant at the estimated cost of £4,630 was approved.
	6 November	The recommendations of the assessors for the competition for the design of the new Wexford Bridge were approved and the following awards made:

> First Place – W J L O'Connell, Cork, £500
> Second Place – William Albert Fairhurst, Glasgow, £300
> Third Place – James Joseph Roghan, Dublin, £200.
>
> The assessors were:-
> William F Barry, AMICE, former county engineer
> Professor Henry N Walsh, ME, DIC, MICE
> Mr Nicholas O'Dwyer, BE, MICEI.

1945	5 January	Mr George Aloysius Cannon, Mount St Francis, Dundalk, appointed secretary to Wexford County Council on the recommendation of the Local Appointment Commissioners.
	9 January	Purchase of 288 apple trees, 3-years, half-standard, for road planting at £21.67 per 100 from Messrs Galvin Brothers, Wexford, approved.
	12 January	Scale of charges for council machinery from 1 April 1944 and 1 April 1945 approved:

> Steam drill .... £3.25 per day
> Engine and granulator (large) £4.00 per day
> (small) £3.00 per day
> Engine and stonebreaker .... £3.50 per day

	Compressor drill plant and lorry £5.50 per day
	Roller .... £2.50 per day
	Concrete mixer .... £1.50 per day
	V8 lorry .... £4.50 per day.
	(Increased charges were necessary because of the increased cost of fuel.)
22 January	Directed that an advertisement be inserted in the local newspapers to the effect that the Fire Brigade located with the Shelbourne Co-operative Agricultural Society, Campile, is available to the public should its services ever be required.
22 February	In her monthly report for January 1945, the matron of the County Home showed the numbers in the house at the end of the month were:

Males		171
Females		165
Children,	3-15 years	42
	1 - 3 years	7
	6 months - 1 year	14
	less than 6 months	35
Total		434

9 March	Specification approved and tenders to be invited for the cutting and saving of not less than 1000 tons of turf in Moneer Bog, Mount Leinster, and delivery to the several county institutions at Wexford, Enniscorthy and New Ross.
14 March	Reports of matrons of hospitals: numbers of patients remaining at the end of February 1945:

Grianan Charman	56
Fever Hospital, New Ross	28
District Hospital, New Ross	17

20 March	Salary scales for administrative staff in 1945 were:

County Secretary	£600 - £700
Accountant	£400 - £550
Staff Officer	£400 - £500
Clerical Officer Grade I	£200 - £350
Clerical Officer Grade II	£100 - £250
Clerk-Typist	£100 - £156.

31 March	Revenue Expenditure for Year – £349,951.
	Capital Expenditure for Year – £5,673.
23 April	Contract with Electricity Supply Board for maintenance of public lighting services for the year ending 31 March 1946 for the sum of £177.15 approved.
8 May	Standards to be met in respect of floor area, ceiling height,

		structure, ventilation, lighting, sanitation, exits, fire protection and cloakrooms in applications for dance hall licences approved.
	8 May	Matron's monthly report showing 134 patients, including 10 maternity patients, remaining in the county hospital on 30 April 1945 noted.
	5 June	County Wexford Sheep Dipping Regulations 1945 approved by the county manager.
	5 June	Examination of premises in Bunclody ordered with a view to connection to the council's water and sewerage services preliminary to surfacing the streets in tarmacadam.
	13 October	Tenders invited for laying of watermains in connection with Rosslare Water Supply.
1946	9 January	Approval given to the purchase of 2 'Coleman Flapper' spraying machines, and 4 'Coleman V-type Gritters' at a cost of £1,378.
	11 June	Supplementary loan of £1,230 raised from OPW for 10 house scheme at Kilmuckridge.
	14 June	Purchase of a Bedford Tipper lorry from Messrs Boggans Auto Service for the sum of £737 approved.
	August	The county engineer and assistant engineers vested with the duties of authorised officer under the Fire Brigade Act 1940 with a view to the inspection of all potentially dangerous buildings in the County Health District.
1947	7 March	Contracts for building 18 labourers' cottages (part of a 328-cottage scheme) approved. Houses to be built in EDs of Ardamine, Ballycarney, Tinnacross, Newtownbarry, St Mary's and Enniscorthy Rural. The prices ranged from £565 to £610 each.
	31 March	Revenue Expenditure for Year – £460,927. Capital Expenditure for Year – £10,968.
	21 May	Appointment of Dr Honoria Aughney as County Medical Officer of Health approved on the recommendation of the Local Appointments Commission.
	14 June	Appointment of Mr Seamus Seosamh Ó Gallchóbhair as county accountant with effect from 1 July 1947, approved on the recommendation of the Local Appointments Commission. (Mr Ó Gallchóbhair was later appointed county secretary and served until his death in 1969.)
1948	March	Loan of £10,000 raised from OPW to provide house purchase and building loans.
	31 March	Revenue Expenditure for Year – £523,724. Capital Expenditure for Year – £11,261.
	12 August	Loan of £175,00 raised from OPW for 252 houses under Rural Scheme (Agreement Scheme).
	October	Loan of £50,000 raised from OPW on behalf of Gorey Town

1949	31 March	Commissioners for Cluainín and Fort Road housing schemes. Revenue Expenditure for Year – £586,525. Capital Expenditure for Year – £59,775.
	31 March	The number of houses provided by the council up to this date, under the enabling legislation, was 3,641.
	19 September	Loan of £7,000 raised from OPW for Bunclody Vocational School.
	24 November	Loan of £2,300 raised from OPW to build Courtown public conveniences.
1950	14 February	Loan of £25,000 raised from OPW to provide house purchase and building loans.
	8 May	Loan of £8,000 raised from OPW for 6 houses at Clough and 4 at Taghmon, under Village Scheme.
1951	9 July	Loan of £10,000 raised from OPW on behalf of Gorey Town Commissioners for purchase and repair of 39 houses at Esmond Street.
1952	14 February	Loan of £10,000 raised from OPW for work on St Senan's Hospital.
	16 April	Loan of £26,000 raised from OPW for 6 houses at Ballycanew, 6 at Killinick, 6 at Coolgreany and 8 at Maudlins under Village Scheme 1950.
	17 April	Loan of £25,000 raised from OPW to provide house purchase and building loans.
	10 June	Loan of £2,900 raised from OPW to build dispensary at Bridgetown.
	15 October	Loan of £10,000 raised from OPW for work on St Senan's Hospital (Salville).
1953	19 January	Loan of £13,500 raised from OPW for work on St Senan's Hospital.
	31 March	Revenue Expenditure for Year – £789,895. Capital Expenditure for Year – £240,205. (First time total annual expenditure exceeded £1,000,000.)
	19 May	Loan of £9,000 raised from OPW to build dispensaries at Broadway, Castlebridge, Clonroche, Foulksmills, Murrintown, Oylegate, Pallas and Rosslare Harbour.
	7 July	Loan of £100,000 raised from OPW for 1950 Rural Scheme (Agreement Scheme).
	23 September	Loan of £3,675 raised from OPW on behalf of Gorey Town Commissioners for housing at Fort Road.
1954	31 March	The number of houses provided by the council up to this date, under the enabling legislation, was 4,050.
	31 March	Revenue Expenditure for Year – £925,602. Capital Expenditure for Year – £206,174.
	27 May	Loan of £12,000 raised from OPW for work on St Senan's Hospital.
	9 June	Loan of £12,000 raised from OPW to build dispensary houses

		at Fethard, Killann and Monamolin.
	10 June	Loan of £4,000 raised from OPW for work on St Senan's Hospital.
	13 September	Loan of £1,100 raised from Treasurer for Gorey Town Commissioners for Town Hall site.
1955	31 March	Revenue Expenditure for Year – £1,016,528.
		Capital Expenditure for Year – £213,376.
		(First time annual revenue expenditure exceeded £1,000,000.)
	22 April	Loan of £48,000 raised from OPW for 1953 CPO scheme.
	22 April	Loan of £100,000 raised from OPW for 1953 Agreement Scheme.
	21 July	Loan of £13,850 raised from OPW for 10 houses at Camolin under 1953 Village Scheme.
	10 August	Loan of £1,760 raised from OPW on behalf of Gorey Town Commissioners for housing at Fort Road.
1956	5 January	Loan of £7,500 raised from OPW for Wexford dispensary.
	5 March	Supplementary loan of £6,300 raised from OPW on behalf of Gorey Town Commissioners for housing at Esmonde Street.
	5 July	Loan of £24,000 raised from OPW for Taghmon water supply.
	16 July	Loan of £100,500 raised from OPW for 1955 Agreement Scheme.
	16 July	Loan of £29,730 raised from OPW for 1954 CPO scheme.
	8 October	Supplementary loan of £1,200 raised from Treasurer to complete dispensary houses at Fethard, Killann and Monamolin.
	8 October	Loan of £4,700 raised from Treasurer for repairs and improvements to County Hospital.
	20 November	Loan of £60,000 raised from Treasurer for reconstruction of county roads.
1957		Automatic data processing department established. Tabulators used.
		Punchcard unit introduced in accounts dept.
	3 January	Loan of £100,000 raised from Office of Public Works for construction of bridge at Wexford.
	31 January	Loan of £6,000 raised from OPW to provide house purchase and building loans.
	16 April	Loan of £1,175 raised from OPW on behalf of Gorey Town Commissioners for housing at Fort Road.
	28 May	Loan of £13,000 raised from OPW for 1956 Agreement Scheme.
	19 December	Loan of £6,000 raised from Treasurer for improvements to St Senan's Hospital, Enniscorthy.
1958 –'70		North county boundary road to Scarawalsh completed.
1958	7 January	Loan of £3,500 raised from Treasurer for improvements to St John's Hospital, Enniscorthy.
	9 January	Loan of £6,500 raised from OPW for improvements to St John's Hospital, Enniscorthy.

CHRONOLOGY

	16 January	Supplementary loan of £8,500 raised from OPW for 1949 Agreement Scheme.
	February	Loan of £7,200 raised from OPW to provide house purchase and building loans.
	26 February	Supplementary loan of £9,000 raised from OPW for 1956 Agreement Scheme.
	30 June	Loan of £128,000 raised from OPW for south regional water supply.
1959		Wexford bridge completed.
	31 March	The number of houses provided by the council up to this date, under the enabling legislation, was 4,417.
	31 July	Loan of £5,000 raised from Treasurer to provide grant to Gorey Leather for disposal of effluent.
	18 August	Loan of £1,560 raised from Treasurer for Rosslare Harbour sewerage scheme.
	27 August	Loan of £3,500 raised from Treasurer for improvements to St Senan's Hospital, Enniscorthy.
	6 October	Supplementary loan of £8,350 raised from OPW for 1958 Village Scheme.
	6 October	Second supplementary loan of £700 raised from OPW for 1949 Agreement Scheme.
	6 October	Supplementary loan of £985 raised from OPW for 1953 Village Scheme.
	25 November	Second supplementary loan of £78,000 raised from OPW for 1956 Agreement.
1960		Rosslare Harbour-Ashfield road scheme.
		New Ross Road - Ballyvergin/Cushenstown scheme.
	February	Loan of £25,000 raised from OPW to provide house purchase and building loans.
	30 June	Loan of £3,750 rasied from OPW for Rectory Road (EY) and Kiltealy water supply.
	12 July	Loan of £16,200 raised from OPW for 1956 CPO scheme.
	11 August	Loan of £2,800 raised from Treasurer for work on St Senan's Hospital.
	30 December	Loan of £1,000 raised from Treasurer to provide house repair loans.
1961	24 February	Loan of £10,000 raised from OPW to build dispensaries at Adamstown, Ballynabola, Ballycullane, Killinick and Whitechurch.
	28 February	Supplementary loan of £3,950 raised from OPW for south regional water supply.
	May	Loan of £35,00 raised from OPW for Taghmon sewerage scheme.
	22 June	Loan of £65,000 raised from Treasurer for road repairs and reconstruction.
	8 July	Loan of £25,000 raised from Treasurer for repairs to cottages.

	27 July	Loan of £38,000 raised from Treasurer for purchase of road machinery.
	25 September	Loan of £78,750 raised from OPW for 1960 Agreement Scheme.
	21 December	Loan of £4,000 raised from OPW for Ballyhogue, Ballymorris and Blackstoops water supply.
1962	22 January	Loan of £65,000 raised from Treasurer for road repairs and reconstruction.
	16 March	Loan of £30,000 raised from OPW to provide supplementary housing grants.
	22 August	Loan of £25,000 raised from Treasurer for repairs to cottages.
	26 November	Loan of £15,000 raised from OPW to provide house purchase and building loans.
	17 December	Loan of £10,000 raised from Treasurer for purchase of fire equipment.
1963	22 January	Supplementary loan of £20,600 raised from OPW for construction of bridge at Wexford.
	26 January	Loan of £11,000 raised from Treasurer for repairs to cottages.
	22 February	Loan of £35,000 raised from Treasurer for road repairs and recostruction.
	6 March	Loan of £16,000 raised from OPW for Bunclody water supply.
	15 March	Loan of £7,500 from Treasurer for work on County Hall.
	26 March	Loan of £10,000 from OPW for Coolgreany sewerage scheme.
	3 May	Loan of £25,000 raised from Treasurer for repairs to cottages.
	8 May	Loan of £100,000 raised from OPW for work on St Senan's Hospital.
	13 May	Loan of £35,000 raised from OPW to provide supplementary housing grants.
	21 May	Loan of £40,000 raised from OPW for Gorey regional water supply.
	20 July	Loan of £300,000 raised from OPW for Kilmore water scheme.
	23 October	Loan of £4,000 raised from OPW for Ferrymountgarrett water supply.
	9 December	Loan of £15,000 raised from Treasurer for repairs to cottages.
1964	January	Loan of £4,500 raised from Treasurer for Glynn water supply.
	24 February	Loan of £20,000 raised from OPW for Bridgetown Vocational School.
	25 March	Loan of £24,000 raised from Treasurer for Enniscorthy dispensary.
	31 March	The number of houses provided by the council up to this date, under the enabling legislation, was 4,546.
	14 May	Loan of £4,500 raised from Treasurer to build Curracloe public conveniences.
	14 May	Loan of £35,000 raised from OPW to provide supplementary housing grants.
	21 May	Loan of £2,800 raised from Treasurer to build Gorey public conveniences.

	6 June	Loan of £35,000 raised from OPW to provide house purchase and building loans.
	15 June	Loan of £1,300 raised from Treasurer for Clonroche sewerage scheme.
	27 June	Loan of £36,450 raised from Treasurer for the purchase of road machinery.
	30 June	Loan of £50,000 raised from Treasurer for road repairs and reconstruction.
	9 July	Loan of £5,000 raised from Treasurer to provide supplementary water and sewage grants.
	21 July	Loan of £3,000 raised from Treasurer for work on District and Fever Hospitals.
	24 July	Loan of £20,000 from OPW for Gorey sewerage scheme.
	28 July	Loan of £11,500 raised from OPW for Fethard sewerage scheme.
	30 July	Loan of £16,000 from OPW for Campile sewerage scheme.
	30 July	Loan of £9,500 raised from OPW for Duncannon sewerage scheme.
	3 September	Loan of £210,000 raised from OPW for south regional water supply.
	17 September	Loan of £1,000 raised from Treasurer to provide house repair loans.
	29 September	Loan of £11,300 raised from OPW for south regional water supply.
	19 October	Loan of £36,900 raised from OPW for south regional water supply.
	23 December	Loan of £56,000 raised from OPW for work on St Senan's Hospital.
1965	19 January	Loan of £1,500 raised from Treasurer for Rosslare Strand water supply.
	19 January	Loan of £5,600 raised from Treasurer for purchase of fire appliance.
	2 March	Loan of £50,000 raised from Treasurer for repairs to cottages.
	12 March	Loan of £11,000 raised from OPW for Great Island water supply (amalgamated with Kilmore region).
	16 March	Loan of £7,000 raised from OPW for Clonhaston water supply.
	31 March	Revenue Expenditure for Year – £1,953,875. Capital Expenditure for Year – £650,820. (First time combined revenue and capital expenditure exceeded £2,000,000.)
	12 April	Loan of £14,000 raised from OPW to build dispensaries at Bannow, Camolin, Bree and Killann.
	13 April	Loan of £10,000 raised from OPW for Milehouse water supply.
	6 May	Loan of £50,000 raised from OPW to provide house purchase and building loans.
	6 May	Loan of £50,000 raised from OPW to provide supplementary housing grants.

	10 May	Loan of £10,000 raised from Treasurer to provide supplementary water and sewage grants.
	6 August	Loan of £37,500 raised from Treasurer for repairs to cottages.
	16 September	Loan of £35,000 raised from OPW for Kilmore regional water supply.
	24 September	Supplementary loan of £22,000 raised from OPW for Bridgetown Vocational School.
	24 September	Loan of £25,000 raised from OPW for New Ross Vocational School.
	10 November	Loan of £90,000 raised from OPW for construction of 41 houses and purchase of 1 house.
	7 December	Loan of £50,000 raised from Treasurer for road repairs and reconstruction.
1966	29 March	Loan of £5,500 raised from Treasurer for installation of heating and telephone systems in County Hall.
	31 March	Revenue Expenditure for Year – £2,200,213. Capital Expenditure for Year – £615,487. (First time annual revenue expenditure exceeded £2,000,000.)
	6 May	Loan of £35,000 raised from OPW to provide house purchase and building loans.
	8 July	Loan of £50,200 raised from OPW for house building.
	26 July	Loan of £35,000 raised from OPW to provide supplementary housing grants.
	30 August	Loan of £44,000 raised from OPW for house building in Gorey.
	8 September	Loan of £20,000 raised from Treasurer for repairs to cottages.
	12 September	Loan of £3,000 raised from Treasurer for improvements to County Hall.
	4 October	Loan of £6,826 raised from OPW as contribution to Ballywilliam and Ballymoney group water supply.
	19 October	Loan of £10,000 raised from OPW for Sheilbaggin and Kilmuckridge Vocational Schools.
	20 October	Retirement of Nora Connolly, county librarian.
	20 October	Loan of £52,000 raised from OPW for water supply and sewerage.
	24 October	Loan of £4,500 raised from OPW to provide supplemenatry housing grants.
	24 October	Loan of £20,000 raised from OPW to provide house purchase and building loans.
	23 November	Loan of £15,000 raised from Royal Liver to provide supplementary water and sewage schemes.
	23 November	Loan of £15,000 raised from Royal Liver to provide supplementary housing grants.
1967	23 February	Loan of £70,000 raised from OPW for construction of O'Hanrahan Bridge, New Ross.
	27 February	Opening of O'Hanrahan bridge, New Ross.
	2 March	Loan of £45,000 raised from OPW for 21 houses.
	4 March	Loan of £29,000 raised from OPW for reconstruction of

		County Hospital.
	13 March	Loan of £45,000 raised from OPW to provide house purchase and building loans.
	1 April	Appoinment of Maurice Flynn as county librarian.
	3 April	Loan of £24,000 raised from OPW for 12 houses at Ballygillane and Rosslare Harbour.
	3 April	Loan of £25,000 raised from OPW for 28 houses at French's Field, Gorey.
	12 July	Loan of £16,000 raised from OPW for improvemnets to St John's Hospital, Enniscorthy.
	13 September	Loan of £25,000 raised from Treasurer for road repairs and reconstruction.
	18 September	Loan of £60,000 raised from OPW to provide supplementary housing grants.
	18 September	Loan of £70,000 raised from OPW to provide house purchase and building loans.
	18 October	Loan of £31,000 raised from Treasurer for purchase of road machinery.
	14 November	Loan of £20,000 raised from IPBMI to provide supplementary water and sewage grants.
	16 November	Loan of £90,000 raised from OPW for Great Island water supply.
	30 November	Loan of £21,000 raised from OPW for 10 houses at Bree.
1968	17 January	Loan of £57,500 raised from OPW for work at Kilmore Quay.
	31 January	Loan of £17,500 raised from OPW for Kilmore regional water supply.
	12 February	Loan of £80,000 raised from OPW for work on St Senan's Hospital.
	16 February	Loan of £32,000 raised from OPW for south regional water supply.

New Ross's sixth bridge was jointly designed by Wexford county surveyor J B Farrell and Kilkenny county surveyor P Burtchaell and was opened on 6 August 1969. It was replaced by O'Hanrahan Bridge which opened in February 1967.

	16 February	Supplementary loan of £4,250 raised from OPW for 1960 Agreement Scheme (75 houses).
	27 February	Loan of £8,000 raised from OPW for purchase of land.
	6 March	Loan of £25,000 raised from OPW for 12 houses under 1968 scheme.
	6 March	Loan of £14,600 raised from OPW for 7 houses.
	31 March	Revenue Expenditure for Year – £2,537,472. Capital Expenditure for Year – £577,394. (First time combined annual revenue and capital expenditure exceeded £3,000,000.)
	14 May	Loan of £7,500 raised from OPW for New Ross and Adamstown Vocational Schools.
	14 May	Loan of £42,000 raised from OPW for Gorey, Enniscorthy, Kilmuckridge, Sheilbaggin, and Bunclody Vocational schools.
1969		Wexford branch library moved to prefabricated building in Hill Street, Wexford.
	14 January	Loan of £22,000 raised from IPBMI for public conveniences at Duncannon, Carne, Blackwater and Ferns.
	21 February	Loan of £50,000 raised from National Bank of Ireland for reconstruction of county roads.
	31 March	The number of houses provided by the council up to this date, under the enabling legislation, was 4,650.
	10 April	Loan of £18,000 raised from OPW for Rosslare-Tagoat water supply.
	21 April	Loan of £140,000 raised from OPW for Gorey/Courtown water supply.
	6 October	Loan of £74,600 raised from OPW for Ferns Housing Scheme.
	23 October	Loan of £52,750 raised from OPW for 23 houses.
	8 December	Loan of £120,000 raised from OPW to provide house purchase and building loans.
	29 December	Loan of £65,000 raised from OPW for work on St Senan's Hospital.
1970		New Ross relief road scheme.
	5 January	Loan of £20,000 raised from Treasurer to provide supplementary water and sewage grants.
	17 January	Loan of £75,000 raised from OPW to provide supplementary housing grants.
	5 March	Loan of £20,000 raised from OPW for Rectory Road (EY) sewerage scheme.
	3 April	Loan of £18,500 raised from OPW for 6 houses at Taghmon.
	21 April	Loan raised from OPW for 6 houses at Ballyhack.
	12 June	Loan of £20,000 raised from Royal Liver to provide supplementary water and sewage grants.
	7 July	Resignation of county librarian, Maurice Flynn.
	18 October	Loan of £10,000 raised from IPBMI to provide supplementary water and sewage grants.

Removing quartzite outcrop at Rocklands, Wexford, during widening of Wexford-Rosslare road, July 1970.

1971	1 September	Appointment of Catherine O'Rourke as county librarian.
1972 –'75		Bunclody/Enniscorthy road – Clohamon-Coolattin; Tombrick-Farmleigh; Farmleigh-Coolnahorna road scheme.
1972		All computer systems designed in-house using COBOL and RPG2, including payroll, expenditure, receipts, creditors, rents, rates, loans, water charges, planning, stores and plant. First mini-mainframe computer – ICL-2903.
		Templescoby-NewRoss/Enniscorthy road scheme.
1974		Rate in the pound = £5.25.
	31 December	The number of houses provided by the council up to this date, under the enabling legislation, was 5,145.
1975		New Ross road – Ballymacar/Cushenstown scheme.
		Ballymackessy – New Ross/Enniscorthy road scheme.
1976	11 October	Opening of new Scarawalsh bridge.
1977	14 February	Foundation stone laid for new Engineers Building.
1979		Bunclody to Clohamon road scheme.
		Rosslare road – Ashfield/Drinagh improvement scheme.
	31 December	The number of houses provided by the council up to this date, under the enabling legislation, was 5,886.
1980		Multi-user online systems distributed on new mainframe computer (ICL-ME29). Area offices come online via Wide Area Network.
		Launch of mobile library service.
	14 November	Official opening of Ferrycarrig bridge.
1981		Official opening of new branch library at Barrack Lane, New Ross.

Vehicles negotiating obstructions on Ferrycarrig bridge in the mid 1970s. The obstructions worked to lighten the load on the deteriorating bridge (which had been built by the council 1910–1912) by reducing traffic flow to a single lane and preventing large, heavy vehicles from crossing.

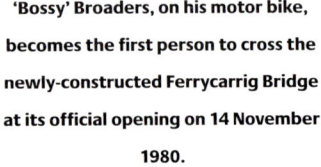

'Bossy' Broaders, on his motor bike, becomes the first person to cross the newly-constructed Ferrycarrig Bridge at its official opening on 14 November 1980.

CHRONOLOGY

		Completion of road from New Ross to Ballymacar.
1982		Completion of improvements to New Ross quays.
	October	New Ross Fire Station becomes operational.
1983		First PCs introduced. CPM operating system (pre-DOS). Word processing, spreadsheet and database applications.
		Index of driving licence records computerised.
1984		Networked departmental systems introduced on DRS300 LAN.
	31 December	The number of houses provided by the council up to this date, under the enabling legislation, was 6,454.
1985		First computerised election count results with public display.
1987	12 January	Official opening of new branch library and headquarters at Wexford.
	June	Irish National Heritage Park, Ferrycarrig, opened by President Patrick Hillery.
	8 September	New fire station in Gorey opens.
1988		Total warrant for collection = £1,871,763.
		First portable hand-held computers for revenue collectors.
1989		Computerisation of all motor taxation and driver licensing records and transactions.
		Unix servers introduced. First integrated organisational office automation (Office Power). First corporate systems redesigned in-house using Relational Database Environment (Ingres).
		Major upgrading and refurbishment of motor taxation office at County Hall, Wexford.
	31 December	The number of houses provided by the council up to this date, under the enabling legislation, was 6,758.
1991		Rafter Bridge, Enniscorthy, opens.
	8 August	Reopening of refurbished front building at County Hall.
1992		INTEGRA integrated financial package implemented. In-house business systems redesigned to integrate with INTEGRA financial modules.
1994		The National Standards Authority of Ireland certifies that Wexford Motor Taxation Office is registered in compliance with Quality System IS ENISO 9002:1994.
		Extension of Motor Taxation and Driver Licensing Department at County Hall, Wexford.
	24 January	Official opening of new branch library at Lymington Road, Enniscorthy.
	9 May	Opening of refurbished administration block and pedestrian link at County Hall.
	31 December	The number of houses provided by the council up to this date, under the enabling legislation, was 6,989.
1995	January	Introduction of PACIS – Planning and Control Information System.
	July	Resort renewal designation.

1996	September	Retirement of county librarian, Catherine O'Rourke. Website, Wexford.ie, first published.
	8 November	Enniscorthy Fire Station opens.
	13 November	Appointment of Fionnuala Hanrahan as county librarian.
	20 December	Received 2000th planning application in one year.
1997		Launch of new mobile library service.
		Year 2000 plan formulated. Systems redesigned for added value.
	22 November	Opening of reconstructed Wexford bridge.
	31 December	The number of houses provided by the council up to this date, under the enabling legislation, was 7,300.
1998		Officepower replaced with MS Exchange and MS Office.
		National Vehicle and Driver system piloted in Wexford.
		Total warrant for collection = £5,501,192.
		Complete upgrade of Network and Desktop PCs to Windows NT4. Wide Area Network upgraded to 64K lines with ISDN backup.
	April	Planning department moves to new ground-floor premises in County Hall.
	5 June	National 1798 Visitor Centre opened by An Taoiseach, Bertie Ahern.
1999		Rate in the pound = £42.54.
		Opening of Cyberskills complex at Westgate, Wexford town.
		OfficePower replaced with MS Exchange and MS Office.
		Computerisation of library service begins.

CHRONOLOGY

New reception area, County Hall, completed 1991.

Section of Sli Charman, County Wexford's coastal path, at Carne.

APPENDIX IV

Wexford County Council Archives

THE COUNCIL MAINTAINS AN ARCHIVE of its own and its predecessors' records. They are available for consultation and research by appointment only and through the Wexford branch of the council's public library service.

GRAND JURY

County Wexford schedule of applications for presentments: 1846-48; 1857-59; 1863-65; 1897-99

County Wexford abstracts and schedules of presentments to the Grand Jury: 1866-67; 1870-72; 1875; 1878; 1881-82; 1886-93; 1895-99

BOARDS OF GUARDIANS

County Wexford:	Poor Law Commissioners' circulars, 1851-52; 1855
Enniscorthy Union:	Minute books, 20 March 1840 to 26 March 1920
	Poor Law Commissioners' Letters, 1846-47; 1853; 1859; 1861-63; 1868-69; 1870-71
	Enniscorthy Union Commissioners' sealed orders and letters, 22 January 1840
	Enniscorthy Union Local Government Board letters, 6 January 1875 to 30 December 1876
Gorey Union:	Minute books, 21 January 1843 to 1 March 1919
	Poor Law Commissioners' letters, 1848; 1849-54; 1858-61
	Poor Law Commissioners' reports, 1864
	Gorey Union letters, December 1910 to April 1911; March to July 1915; January to June 1917
	Gorey Union requisitions, April 1866 - March 1897
	Gorey Union quarterly meetings, April 1899 - November 1824
	Gorey Medical Dispensary Minute book, March 1852 - February 1899
New Ross Union:	Minute books, 27 March 1844 to 22 April 1922
Wexford Union:	Minute books, 1 August 1840 to 6 May 1922
	Veterinary inspector's book, December 1878 - April 1884
	Letters to Local Government Board, August 1897 - July 1898

Wexford Infirmary books, May 1845 - December 1845; July 1908 - August 1923

Wexford Dispensary management committee book, March 1852 - May 1868

Wexford Dispensary minute book, January 1868 - April 1899

Rural District Councils

Enniscorthy RDC Minute books, 4 May 1899 to 12 May 1920

Enniscorthy Contracts Ledger – special works, April 1914 - June 1925

Gorey RDC Minute books, 27 January 1900 to 13 June 1925

New Ross RDC Minute books, 10 April 1899 to 17 August 1925

Wexford RDC Minute books, 5 August 1899 to 10 April 1920

County Council

Minutes of Council meetings, 22 April 1899 -

Finance Committee, April 1899 - May 1943

County Managers' Orders, August 1942 -

Board of Health and Public Assistance Minute books, November 1921 - July 1942

APPENDIX V

Wexford County Council Publications – a select bibliography

[The] *Arts in the classroom initiative report*, 1998

Building sensitively in the landscapes of County Wexford, 1988, School of Architecture, UCD for Wexford County Council, ISBN: 1 870089 15 4

Celebrating 100 years of community service: 1999 Wexford County Council calendar, 1998

Commemorating 1798: 1998 Wexford County Council calendar, 1997

County Wexford Local Authorities 5 year report, 1974-1979, 1980

County Wexford Tourism holiday activities in County Wexford, 1992

Crainn i Loch Garman, 1991

Discover Wexford, 1997, Wexford Tourism

Edermine Ireland: a unique site in a unique location

Envirowex, 1991-

Exploring 1798: an introduction to sources and an educational pack for students, 1998, Wexford County Council Schools Library Service, ISBN: 0 9519800 1 7

[A] *Guide to nature at Curracloe*, 1992, ISBN: 0 9519800 0 9

Guide to the functions and records of Wexford County Council, 1998

Guide to the rules and practices of Wexford County Council, 1998

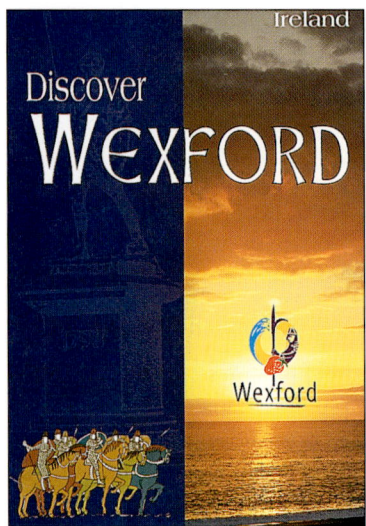  

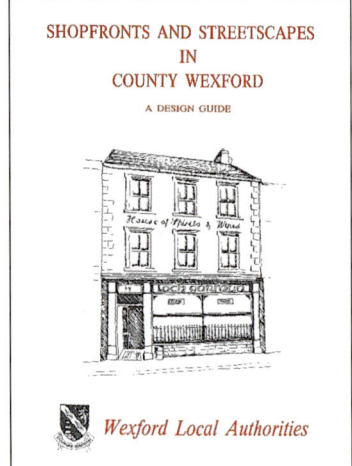

Mightier than the sword: the culture of County Wexford revealed through its histories, 1998, Wexford County Council Public Libraries
Official guide to County Wexford, 1984, Condor Publishing
186 years of Ferrycarrig bridges, 1980
Recyclers' guide to County Wexford, 1996
[A] Review of local government, 1979-1985, 1985
Shopfronts and streetscapes in County Wexford, a design guide, 1991, Wexford Local Authorities
Slí Charman: Wexford's coastal path
Thatched cottages in Kilmore Quay
Tourism development strategy for County Wexford, 1996
Water Quality Management Plan for River Slaney catchment including the estuary, 1986, Wexford, Carlow and Wicklow County Councils
Wexford coastline coastal management plan, 1992
Wexford County Council annual report, 1991 -
Wexford County Council election results, 1985
Wexford County Council election results, 1991
Wexford County Council strategy statement 1998-2001, 1998
Wexford County Enterprise action plan, 1998
Wexford Ireland, 1997